E APELOIG FE

EPHEN DOYLE VINCE FROST KIT

OGNA MARGO CHAS

R ISLEY STEVE LISKA EMILY OBE

ER FRITZ GOTTSCH

ER BONNIE SIEGLER MICHAEL STR

ON MICHAEL JOHNS

T CROSBY STEPHEN DOYLE VINC

DITI KATONA LUCIC

AN ALEXANDER ISLEY STEVE LISK

R MARISCAL DEBBI

PAULA SCHER BONNIE SIEGLER

MASTERS OF DESIGN
LOGOS & IDENTITY

ROCKPORT

First published in the United States of America by
Rockport Publishers, a member of
Quayside Publishing Group
100 Cummings Center
Suite 406-L
Beverly, Massachusetts 01915-6101
Telephone: (978) 282-9590
Fax: (978) 283-2742
www.rockpub.com

Library of Congress Cataloging-in-Publication Data
Adams, Sean.
  Masters of design : logos and identity : learn from twenty designers who have changed the logo land-scape / Sean Adams.
     p. cm.
  Includes bibliographical references.
  ISBN 1-59253-441-4
  1. Logos (Symbols)--Design. 2. Industrial design coordination. I. Title.

NC1002.L63A32 2008
741.6--dc22
                          2008000583

ISBN-13: 978-1-59253-441-8
ISBN-10: 1-59253-441-4

10 9 8 7 6 5 4 3 2 1

Design: AdamsMorioka

Printed in China

A COLLECTIVE OF THE WORLD'S MOST INSPIRING LOGO DESIGNERS

SEAN ADAMS

MASTERS OF DESIGN LOGOS & IDENTITY

BEVERLY MASSACHUSETTS

ROCKPORT PUBLISHERS

CONTENTS

Crosby Associates, Chicago, Illinois, U.S.A.
Liska + Associates, Chicago, Illinois, U.S.A.

Concrete Design Communications, Toronto, Ontario, Canada

Modern Dog, Seattle, Washington, U.S.A.

Alexander Isley Inc., Redding, Connecticut, U.S.A.

Morla Design, San Francisco, California, U.S.A.
Pentagram, San Francisco, California, U.S.A.

AdamsMorioka, Inc., Beverly Hills, California, U.S.A.
Chase Design Group, Los Angeles, California, U.S.A.
Ph.D, Santa Monica, California, U.S.A.

C&G Partners, New York, New York, U.S.A.
Doyle Partners, New York, New York, U.S.A.
Mucca Design, New York, New York, U.S.A.

Number Seventeen, New York, New York, U.S.A.
Pentagram, New York, New York, U.S.A.
Sterling Brands, New York, New York, U.S.A.

Felix Beltran & Asociados, Mexico City, Mexico

Willoughby Design Group, Kansas City, Missouri, U.S.A.

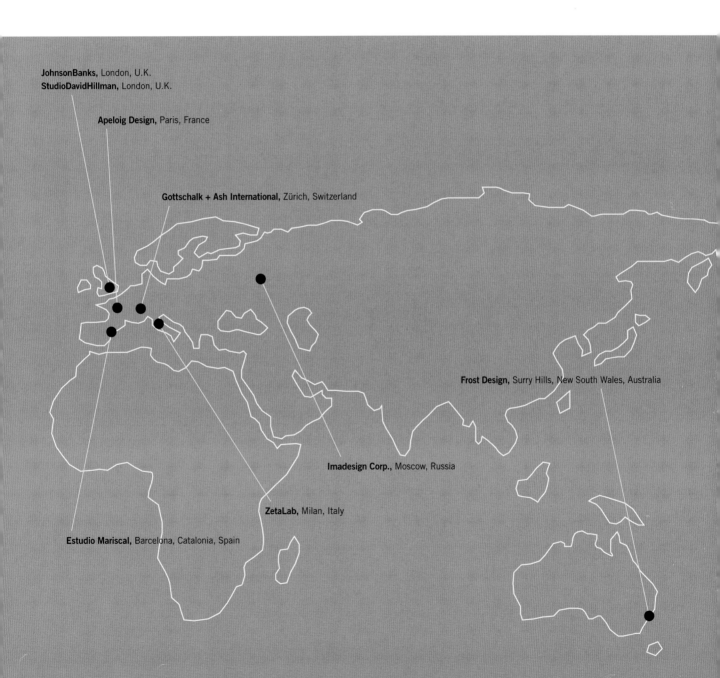

JohnsonBanks, London, U.K.
StudioDavidHillman, London, U.K.

Apeloig Design, Paris, France

Gottschalk + Ash International, Zürich, Switzerland

Frost Design, Surry Hills, New South Wales, Australia

Imadesign Corp., Moscow, Russia

ZetaLab, Milan, Italy

Estudio Mariscal, Barcelona, Catalonia, Spain

A "master," in the context of design, is a person whose work serves as a model or idea to the profession. If we refine this idea in the making of logos, we look at individuals who have contributed to the form, concept, and standards of excellence in identity design. Many masters have enhanced the practice of logo design or identity systems. Among this varied group of designers and design firms, Paul Rand, Saul Bass, Chermayeff and Geismar, William Golden, Massimo Vignelli, and Pentagram have contributed to design and society with the creation of some of the world's most recognizable logos. Over the past two decades, a new group of designers has influenced the profession with a broad focus across many media.

The impulse to identify with symbols or letters has been a common thread for more than 5,000 years. The earliest marks determined ownership of an Egyptian brick. The Industrial Revolution saw an explosion of logos as mass-produced products flooded the marketplace. Today, the logo is in the middle of another major transition. The static logos and rigid visual systems no longer function in a multiplatform environment. This, coupled with the audience's enormous amount of daily visual input, has created a need for logos to evolve. The masters of logo design today address this issue in many ways. While they share common values of clear communication and excellence in craft, the approach to issues of multiplatform thinking are widely varied.

The client's needs and communication are the foundation for any identity system. Once determined, the logo may be applied to anything from a stationery system to a mobile phone screen. It may need to move, have accompanying audio cues, or change proportion. Solving these issues requires not only the ability to make a clear and memorable logo, but to also think four-dimensionally. Space and time are now criteria that are considered. The visual system is flexible and able to evolve. A flat, one-color logo, and visual system of a blue bar and one typeface may be inviting. This system, however, will fail in today's complex environment.

A common theme appeared when compiling the work of the twenty masters in this book. The logos shared a sense of effortlessness, and lightness. There were no overworked marks; no marks sinking under the weight of their own importance. Most great works of art and design appear to be the only logical choice, simple to create. When looking at a Picasso in a museum, many viewers think, "I could have done that." But, of course, they didn't. The sense of ease and playfulness is one of the reasons for its success. Another theme was the clear concept of the designer and the public good. All of the designers expressed their desire to make the world a better place, to solve a client's problem and help the larger culture. The optimism inherent in these ideas is a defining aspect of these masters.

At the end of the day, it is our job as designers to help someone. We make a logo that will help a product or service succeed, or we design a visual system that will create inspiration. The logo is the distillation of the client's most basic communication, "This is who I am." The visual system answers the question, "This is what I believe." The combination of the two, as offered in this book, by twenty seven of the world's masters of design, creates a message that is exciting, clear, and potent.

A logo is not a brand, unless it's on a cow.

The verbiage used in the creation of logos is a modern Tower of Babel. Terms such as *identity*, *symbol*, *mark*, *word mark*, and *identity system* have different meanings, depending on whom you talk to. Here are the terms as defined and referred to in this book.

What Does a Logo Do?

A logo can answer these questions:

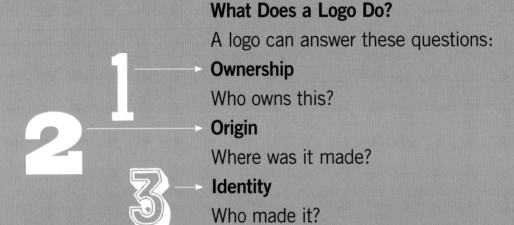

Ownership
Who owns this?

Origin
Where was it made?

Identity
Who made it?

It can:

Differentiate from competition

Create a focus internally

Provide clear identification

Enable the audience to form a personal relationship

Create merchandising opportunities

Create credibility

Bring order to chaos

Communicate the message

Logo:
A distinctive symbol representing a company, object, publication, person, service, or idea.

Mark:
A recognizable symbol used to indicate ownership or origin of goods.

Trademark:
A name or symbol used to show that a product is made by a particular company and legally registered.

Signature:
A distinctive mark, or combination of visual forms. A graphics standards manual may call for the "signature" to be applied to all brochures. This is simply a synonym for "logo."

Word mark:
A word mark uses the company name with proprietary typography and letterforms.

The advantage of word marks is that the enormous amount of logos in the current environment has made recognition of symbols difficult. Using the entire name spelled out sidesteps the problem of recognition.

The disadvantage of word marks is that if not handled skillfully, a word mark alone may be generic and lack mnemonic value.

Symbol:
The symbol is the iconic portion of a logo, such as the Chase Manhattan Bank symbol, the Cingular man, and the Time Warner Cable eye/ear. At times the symbol may exist without the word mark, for example, the Nike swoosh, Apple's apple, and the CBS eye.

The benefit of using a symbol alone follows the idea that "a picture is worth a thousand words." However, if the symbol is separated from the word mark and the mark does not have equity, it may be difficult to recognize.

Monogram:
A design of one or more letters, usually the initials of a name, used to identify a company, publication, person, object, or idea.

The monogram solves mnemonic and legibility issues. However, monograms are often masquerading as logos. Generic initials treated in clever ways may look better on towels or glasses than on a corporate business card. Initials woven together have very little meaning. Most monogram logos depend on large-scale audience contact and repeated viewing for recognition.

Identity:
The combination of the logo, visual system (typeface, colors, imagery), and editorial tone form a unique and cohesive message for a company, person, object, or idea.

Brand:
The identity is not a brand. The brand is the perception formed by the audience about a company, person, or idea. This perception is the culmination of logo, visuals, identity program, messages, products, and actions. A designer cannot "make" a brand. Only the audience can do this. The designer forms the foundation of the message with the logo and identity system.

Jahresausstellung 2005

Die Ausstellung zeigt Arbeiten von Studentinnen und Studenten aus den Fächern »Entwurf«, »Entwerfen und Konstruieren«, »Bildnerisches Gestalten«, die während des Semesters, innerhalb eines Austauschprogramms oder als Diplomarbeit im vergangenen Jahr entstanden sind.

Das Institut für Geschichte und Theorie der Architektur (gta); das Institut für Hochbautechnik (IHBT); das Institut für Denkmalpflege (ID) sowie das Netzwerk Stadt und Landschaft (NSL) mit dem Studio Basel/Institut der Gegenwart, dem Institut für Städtebau (ISB) und dem Institut für Landschaftsarchitektur (ILA) präsentieren ebenfalls ausgewählte Arbeiten aus Lehre und Forschung, um die Vielfalt der Ansätze und Disziplinen zu dokumentieren, die unsere Schule auszeichnet.

Ausstellungseröffnung
Donnerstag, 27. Oktober 2005,
18.00 Uhr
Eingangshalle,
Gebäude HIL D 30
ETH Hönggerberg
CH-8093 Zürich

Öffnungszeiten
28. Oktober bis 25. November
Montag bis Freitag,
7.00 bis 22.00 Uhr
Samstag, 8.00 bis 12.00 Uhr
Sonntag geschlossen

DARCH
Departement Architektur

ETH
Eidgenössische Technische Hochschule Zürich
Swiss Federal Institute of Technology Zürich

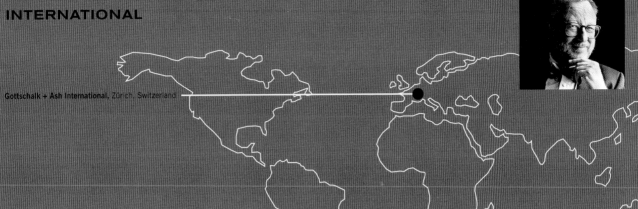

Gottschalk + Ash International, Zürich, Switzerland

Certain logos are laughably dated. We look at them and find them nostalgic, or quaint. From the cartoon mascots of the 1960s to the psychedelic forms of a 1970s brand logo, they all share the attribute of being locked in a specific time. Design is not Darwinian. That is, it does not evolve and become "better" with each generation. Design is a product of its time and place. Longevity is an attribute that Gottschalk + Ash infuse into every identity project. Partner Fritz Gottschalk explains, "A logo must be timeless in thinking and appearance."

OPPOSITE
The identity design for the Department of Architecture at ETH Zürich, a noted science and technology university, uses a specific visual language in addition to its logo.

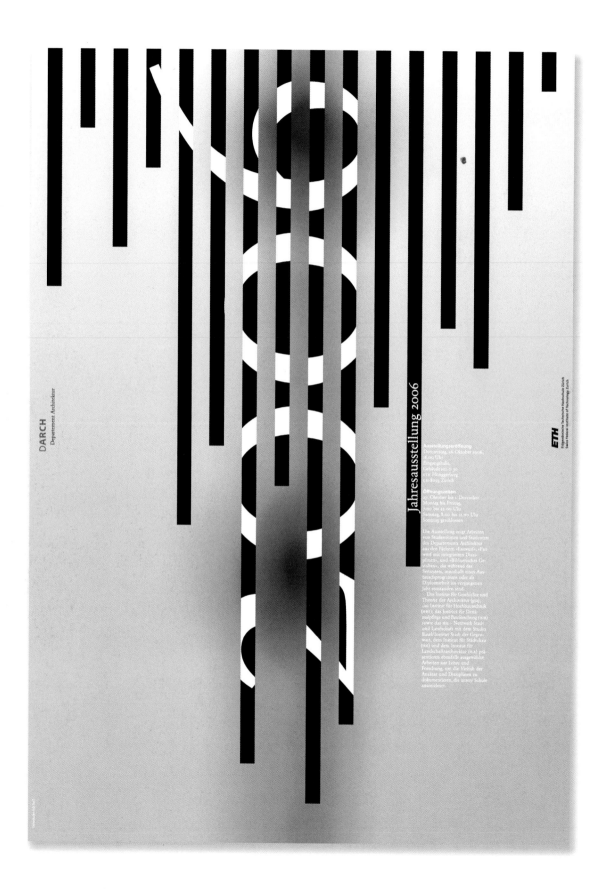

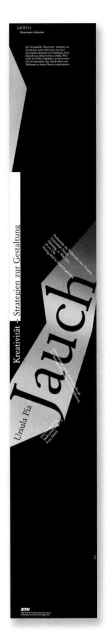

THIS SPREAD
The strong monochromatic
palette, simple typography,
and bold use of scale and
space define the visual
language of the Department
of Architecture at ETH
Zürich on the opposite
poster and for the series
of banners on this page.
The proprietary aspect
of the identity is reinforced
with consistent usage
of a simple system.

For more than forty years, Gottschalk + Ash has created logos and identity systems that remain timeless. This timeless quality is a result of two components: a strategic imperative to create clear and powerful communications and an adherence to the principles of modernism, specifically, simplicity. When asked about his primary philosophy on logos, Gottschalk responds plainly, "Keep it simple."

Process

The team at Gottschalk + Ash, partners, Fritz Gottschalk, and Sascha Loetscher, and executive designers, Michael Kahn and Michel Schmid begin every identity project with brand research. Strategic communication is at the heart of the success of his work. This research explores the target audience's motivations and perceptions. While this is not unusual in an identity process, Gottschalk adds the layer of feelings. In some design circles, where logic and rational thinking drive all decisions, this would be heresy. But Gottschalk believes that emotions are a strong driver in decision making, and the success or failure of a logo. The component of emotional response is a minefield. The designer has left the safe waters of rational and measurable criteria and has entered a place where every person will respond differently, and often inexplicably. But this emotional connection is the piece that makes the difference between a flat and unremarkable logo, and a successful and memorable logo.

Gottschalk's identity work incorporates not just well crafted form, but the naming and visual expression. As technology advances, and the means of communication change, the name becomes even more critical. There are instances where a logo will not work, such as an on-air cable guide, or mobile phone message. Gottschalk states, "Effective names help to express the essence of a company or product and differentiate it in a crowded marketplace." His process to develop a proprietary name encompasses the communication issues, formal components of a word, and an approach that ensures a name that resonates in many languages on a global scale.

Brand architecture is an integral ingredient of Gottschalk's process. As companies expand and evolve, the logo is often the first element to lose cohesion. One department adopts the primary logo, but changes the color, while another adds a secondary name in a random typeface. A merger or acquisition creates even more confusion. Seemingly innocuous changes eventually erode all equity in a logo. Gottschalk addresses both the visual structure internally, and the logo usage, and a transition strategy that helps a brand, in his words, "Keep current and in-line with the corporate vision."

Longevity

Gottschalk + Ash's long success can be ascribed to its revolutionary thinking, and also to its commitment to craft. Every curve, letterform, color, and shape is refined repeatedly until it is, "Harmonious, concise, containing a cognitive element, and able to withstand wear and tear," says Gottschalk. The logo for Ciba embodies this. The challenge was to create a global brand and launch it in 117 countries simultaneously. A new name was created as well as full brand implementation, new brand management tools, and an internal communication program. The final name and butterfly symbol communicate the power of transformation. The forms used, from a repeat of a perfect circle to harmonious letterforms, work together to create a logo that has mnemonic value and visual impact. This, combined with the emotive qualities of transformation, create equity and power.

"Too flashy, too fashionable, and too ephemeral," are attributes that are common to logos that fail. This echoes some of Gottschalk's sentiments on long-lived and timeless logos. While a logo that uses the most current and exciting typeface, or colors that represent a current attitude or style, may have initial appeal, it will quickly become tied to the era of its creation. The logo is not the only element that can become, in Gottschalk's terms, "Too flashy." His approach also addresses

S 2 1

The Sponsors' Voice

S 21
Marketing Communication
Koeniginstr. 28
80802 Munich
Germany

P +49 89 3800 19538
F +49 89 3800 18625

www.s21.com

Musterfirma
Herrn Dr. Peter Mustermann
Corporate Communications
Musterstrasse 112
80802 München

SPONSORING MÜNCHNER PHILHARMONIKER

Erhöhung von Effektivität und Effizienz im Sponsoring

Lorem ipsum dolor sit amet, consectetuer adipiscing elit, sed diam
nonummy nibh euismod tincidunt ut laoreet dolore magna aliquam
erat volutpat. Ut isi enim ad minim veniam, quis nos trud exerci-
tation ullamcorper suscipit lobortis nisl ut aliquip ex ea commodo consequat. Duis autem vel eum iriure dolor in hendrerit in
vulputate velit esse molestie consequat, vel illum dolore eu feu-
giat nulla facilisis at vero eros et ac cumsan et iusto odio
dignissim qui blandit praesent luptatum zzril delenit augue duis
dolore te feugait nulla facilisi.

Lorem ipsum dolor sit amet, consectetuer adipiscing elit, sed
diam nonummy nibh euismod tincidunt ut laoreet dolo re magna aliquam erat volutpat. Ut isi enim ad minim veniam, quis nostrud
exerci tation ullamcorper suscipit lobortis nisl ut aliquip ex
ea commodo consequat.

Mit freundlichen Grüssen
Dr. M. Mustermann

Top Five Logo Design Rules

Logos must:

1. Be harmonious
2. Be concise
3. Contain a cognitive element
4. Withstand wear and tear
5. Be timeless

OPPOSITE
Supplemental icons
delineate functional
information such as
restrooms, and medical
specific fields such as
Cardiology. The complex
subject matter is simpli-
fied to be universally
understandable.

LEFT
The letterhead design
for S20, an organization
of 20+ major German
sponsors, exemplifies
the clarity of Gottschalk +
Ash's identity philosophy.
No extraneous elements
are used. The letterhead
is functional, even providing guides for folding.
The identity is given
dominance, allowing for
maximum recognition
and legibility.

Ciba

THIS PAGE
Ciba is a global leader dedicated to producing high-value effects for its customers' products. These add performance, protection, color, and strength to plastics, paper, automobiles, buildings, and home and personal care products. The identity uses the recognizable symbol of a butterfly which symbolizes transformation, beauty, and pollination. The icon can also be used as an abstract graphic of multi-colored dots such as these banners.

weissbooks.w

THIS PAGE
A one color word mark is the logo for weissbooks.w, a new German publisher. The addition of ".w" after "weissbooks" hints at the contemporary nature of the company, founded in the time of the internet. The letterforms retain a friendly, but precise quality. The choice of a word mark rather than an icon is based on the client's business. As publishers, weissbooks.w lives in the world of the printed word.

Andreas Höfele
Abweg
Eine Erzählung

Gisela Getty
Jutta Winkelmann
Jamal Tuschick
Die Zwillinge
oder Vom Versuch
Geist und Geld zu küssen

Jacqueline Moser
Lose Tage
Roman

Marlene Streeruwitz
Der Abend nach
dem Begräbnis
der besten Freundin.

E. M. Cioran
Aufzeichnungen
aus Talamanca

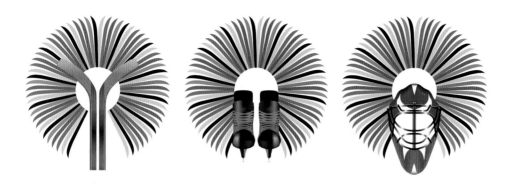

100 Years of International Ice Hockey   100 Years of International Ice Hockey

UBS   UBS

"Have lunch with management."

—Fritz Gottschalk, partner, Gottschalk + Ash International

the visual components of an identity system. The individual components can easily be corrupted, and lose their equity, by lack of control. Often, the responsibility of implementation of an identity system will be given to Gottschalk + Ash. However, when other creative partners are involved, Gottschalk creates a manual for usage.

A manual can provide the rules and guidelines for usage, but it is useless without compliance. "Besides a manual, endorsement by top management—someone who maintains continuity—is important," says Gottschalk. This is easier said than done. Typically upper management is populated by business, not creative, individuals. Understanding the value of the logo is one component. Believing that it should not be violated and instead should be used consistently is essential to Gottschalk's philosophy on logos and visual systems. "The most challenging aspect of any logo project is the involvement of management. Have lunch with them," is his advice.

The strength and stability of Gottschalk's logos would indicate a preference for repeat and expected applications of the logo. The truth is one of the attributes that sets him apart as one of the world's best logo designers. "Once the identity system is designed and approved, my favorite applications are the ones we've never done before," Gottschalk says. "Anything to do with uncharted waters."

This is exemplified by the system and applications for Labatt Breweries of Canada. Initially, Gottschalk discovered that there were so many variations of the Labatt brand identity in use that legally it would be difficult to protect the Labatt trademark. Gottschalk + Ash unified and gave new depth and resonance to the fragmented identity. They repositioned the company as a global competitor. The varied applications became the vehicles for the brand message. Gottschalk + Ash worked with Labatt to develop an online tool to guide internal staff to more clearly understand the company's brand structure, key messages, and unified communications program.

Gottschalk states, "Good communication has the power to involve, inform, motivate, and sell. It translates visual emotion into images and creates lasting impressions. How an organization is perceived by all of its audiences depends greatly on the effectiveness of the visual translation of the anticipated goals." His work has created many of the guiding principles of logo design. As Gottschalk + Ash enters its fourth decade, Gottschalk has no appearance of decreasing his commitment to excellence. He summarizes his advice and driving conviction: "Never be satisfied."

Equity Toys
A DIVISION OF EQUITY MARKETING INC.

MCA and
Equity Toys
Building
KFC's Kids
Business

*Presented
November 2, 1996*

ALEXANDER ISLEY, INC.

**Alexander Isley
Redding, Connecticut, U.S.A.**

ABOVE
The logo for Equity Toys,
a manufacturer and
distributor of licensed
toys was developed to
work with multiple parts,
Equity Marketing and
its subsidiaries, Equity
Toys and Equity Promo-
tion, and on multiple
types of media from
print to merchandise.

OPPOSITE ABOVE
The logo for BlueBolt
Studio, a software tool
developed for architects
and interior designers
uses the product's pur-
pose to create a visual
system. The software
helps architects and
interior designers review,
specify, and order surface
materials and fabrics.
This is expressed with
the logo's dimensionality.
The trade show booth

BlueBolt
NETWORKS

The Barn Doors Are
OPEN

Stone Barns Center for Food and Agriculture

is OPEN TO THE PUBLIC

COME HELP US **CELEBRATE**

Sunday, May 2, 2004 10 am–5 pm

Rain or Shine

FREE ADMISSION: PLEASE BRING A FRIEND

AND ENJOY

musician **Dan Zanes**

AND

storyteller & musician **Little Hawk**

ALONG WITH
**wool weaving,
fresh-from-the-farm treats,
and sheep shearing**
meet the farmers

**630 Bedford Road, Pocantico Hills, NY
914 366 6200
www.stonebarnscenter.org**

STONE BARNS
CENTER FOR FOOD
& AGRICULTURE™

STONE BARNS
CENTER FOR FOOD
& AGRICULTURE™

STONE BARNS
CENTER FOR FOOD
& AGRICULTURE™

BELOW
The brand-visual equity research for Tropicana showed that the "straw in orange" was the key element in the orange juice category's sea of ubiquitous visual cues.

The identity is designed to reinforce and leverage this equity to create a unified brand icon. This allows the product to be instantly recognizable and proprietary. This also simplified the graphic architecture of multiple products.

Debbie Millman, New York, New York, U.S.A.

Sterling Brands, New York, New York, U.S.A.

In physics, the idea of a grand unification theory is a type of field theory that allows all of the fundamental forces between elementary particles to be written in terms of a single field. If proven, this theory would create a simple and elegant solution that provides one answer. Sterling Brands partner Debbie Millman would not agree with a grand unification theory. "There isn't a 'mass market' to target a product or a company anymore; there is no one demographic picture of the planet," she says.

The evolution of a singular audience to one based on variation is at the center of Millman's concepts on logo design. "I have come to believe that the term 'designing logos' ultimately undermines the job we do as consultants, marketers, designers, and strategists," she explains. Her solution is to redefine the creation of logos and identity.

Related Disciplines

Millman's identities holistically balance four distinct, but related, disciplines: cultural anthropology, behavioral psychology, commerce, and creativity. These disciplines are then expressed visually. Cultural anthropology, whether it is an obsession with social networks, or politics, or the cult of celebrity, has an impact on the audience's interpretation of the world and its place in it. Psychology of the audience—what they are thinking, and why they are thinking it, provides the tools needed to solicit the audience's imagination. Commerce gives an understanding of the marketplace, impact of messages, and perception. Finally, she maintains the impact of creativity. "We include creativity because if we don't create an engaging identity, then consumers won't even see it," she says.

The understanding of the audience's driving forces has contributed to Millman's formal thinking. "Symbols tell a better story and solicit an audience's projective imagination," she explains. "Words suffer from mis-interpretation and a literal, or illiterate audience, but they are better at conveying a specific message." Millman's logos are clear and single-minded. She uses the term, "telegraphic" when discussing the look of a logo. Nevertheless, many logos have become iconic despite a complicated and/or multidimensional expression. The Starbucks logo is a good example. Millman uses the Starbucks logo to communicate the value of consistent marketing and good product. This alludes to one of the maxims of father of modern logo design, Paul Rand, that a good logo can never make a bad product better, but a good logo can make a good product spectacular.

Recognition

Millman expands on the value of consistent marketing with the Nike swoosh as an example. "I can't tell you how many clients have asked Sterling to design the next swoosh. But what are they asking for really?" she asks. The Nike swoosh was designed twenty years ago, in twenty-four hours, by a young art student. She charged $60, and when Nike cofounder Phil Knight saw it, he didn't like it. He wanted the logo to incorporate more action in it, similar to the Adidas logo, which was a popular competitor at the time. Now, after millions

ABOVE
The Tropicana identity system is built on a lockup of all elements. The overlap of the straw in the last *a* of the word mark highlights the importance of the "straw in orange" in all communications. Simplicity is achieved by making the "straw in orange" the hero of the package.

OPPOSITE ABOVE
A series of identities designed for Cablevision's Optimum branded services: digital cable TV, broadband Internet, and digital home voice services. The logo and identity system focus on the communication of core attributes: speed, technology, and ease of use. The identity system leverages contemporary iconic letterforms to appeal to the broad audience of Cablevision's digital services.

Optimum
online

Optimum
voice

interactive
Optimum

RIGHT
The style guide for
Cablevision's Optimum
branded services functions
as a clear set of parameters
and instructions for the
usage of the multiple identities created. The guide
is designed to reflect the
attitude of the brand, and
includes a CD of elements.

of advertising dollars behind it, the swoosh is the world's most popular logo. Millman explains, "But guess what? It happens to be Newport cigarette's logo upside down. It is not necessarily having a type of mark that is critical, it is the marketing and the positioning of the brand with the logo that gives it its power of recognition, and ultimately, its success."

Millman's personal manner is straightforward and clear, with a dose of charm. She conveys a sense of organization and structure. Her conversation about successful logos follows the same focused theme. Millman maintains two rules for success. "You must be courageous and have a strategic focus." Her work creates identity solutions that are intrinsically tied to a clear marketing strategy. "Talk directly, passionately, and as uniquely as possible to your audience," she says. It is the relentless persistence and constant assessment of the logo's relevance to the key constituency that is an ingredient for success.

Millman then discusses the idea of single-minded clarity. "The logo must be a telegraphic expression of the company's positioning, personality, and cultural values, as well as be a symbolic link between your target consumer and the company," she says. This contrasts with her last rule to understand the need for change. Millman asks the client pointed questions

to determine this: What is the dynamic for changing the logo? What is evolutionary or revolutionary change? What is visionary? How far is too far? What are the constructs that are on the brand and how can the vision be redefined? Millman uses the responses to determine the identity's telegraphic expression of the positioning, personality, and cultural values. She concludes, "The identity should fit the client's vision and business strategies, help characterize the organization, and ultimately be a beacon for the viewer in any environment."

A visual system—colors, typography, and imagery—is a vital component of every identity system. Millman's approach creates these items with a strong emphasis on the final form of the logo's applications. She strives to keep clarity at the center of every touch point the identity has with the public. This audience includes internal and external constituents, shareholders, and stakeholders. Visual anomalies in the system are not tolerated. This hard-line on maintenance is not extreme. As Millman states, "If there is not one voice, one message, and one clear, understandable system, you're doomed." Maintaining consistency is the most difficult aspect of an identity project. Logos in isolation, on a plain white piece of paper, look great. A great vision in isolation is easy. A great strategy in isolation is easy. Meeting the extraordinary and daunting challenge, Millman's work links all three—logo, vision, and strategy—seamlessly together.

The Launch

There are great logos sitting in a flat file unused, and there are incredible solutions that existed for a moment before being abandoned. The internal launch within an organization will ensure that everyone involved understands the reason for change, the mechanics of the system, and the plan for the details that others will try to ignore or circumvent. Essentially you want to give no one the opportunity to say "Oh! I didn't realize that."

Millman's ultimate goal for an identity is to reflect the overall culture of the brand, the product, or the company. She uses identity to evoke a unique combination of sensory perceptions communicated through various media and applications. "The extension of any one of our sensory perceptions impacts the way we think and act," she says, "and this affects the way we perceive the brand, or the product, or the company." The strength of Millman's work lies in the understanding that when perceptions change, people change, and the brand is affected. Her logos create value and success for products due to her belief that the discipline of designing logos and identity has more impact on our culture than any other creative medium.

"Talk directly, passionately, and as uniquely as possible to your audience."

—Debbie Millman, Partner, Sterling Brands

Top Seven Rules for Logo Failure

1. A logo that's the front face for an organization that is badly marketed
2. Global logos that do not consider global interpretations
3. Logos that need an explanation
4. Overly "trendy" logos
5. Logos that require complicated production techniques
6. Logos that require in-depth training in which to educate users
7. Logos with multiple taglines or messages that are not always in sync

ESTUDIO MARISCAL

Javier Mariscal, Barcelona, Catalonia, Spain

Estudio Mariscal, Barcelona, Catalonia, Spain

Javier Mariscal's approach comes from the point of view of creating images. His firm, Estudio Mariscal, works in a broad range of media from print to interiors to support the messages of the identities they create. Mariscal expresses himself through a personal language that is complex in its intention and simple in its declaration. The work is often contradictory, innocent, and provocative at the same time. He maintains a commitment to innovation and taking risks with logos and identity systems.

OPPOSITE
The visual identity for the brand Camper for Kids, creates a brand image that positions the product as playful, fun, spontaneous, and irreverent. Applications include posters, packaging, and bags.

Within the work Mariscal produces is an inherent sense of delight, which may seem to be a light touch in a serious corporate setting. This presence of delight, however, is the experience that makes Mariscal's identities fresh, surprising, and memorable.

Well-Tailored Logos

When discussing his philosophy about logos, Mariscal jokes, "Logos are like people. Some you like and become friends with. Others you don't even want to see. The worst part of logos is that they can be very strange guys. They always have the same look, and you can't tell if things are going well or going badly." This humor and touch of wit pervades much of Mariscal's logo work. His process starts with the intent to solve the client's problem and give them an identity that will fit, in his words, like "a tailored suit." Mariscal has a strong visual style that he incorporates into the form of the logos. Typically, his clients come to him because they believe that style will work well with their businesses. A common question among designers is "How did they let you do that?" In the instance of Mariscal's logos, he is clear at the onset that he will solve the problem, create work that will succeed, but he will do what he does. This understanding of his own vision and ability to impart that vision to the client produces a wide range of logos.

Mariscal has a clear preference for symbols as a successful form rather than word marks. He uses the cross as the most potent example. Whether it's the Catholic cross or the *cruz*

THIS SPREAD
The logo for the Camper brand is applied to multiple pieces and uses animation as the primary focus. To create the brand image, the collage technique is applied to the illustrations. The strong color palette and limited typography also create a strong and cohesive identity system.

Camper for Hands is aimed at the Japanese market. The design is applied to the packaging, the advertising and the interior design of the camper shops in Japan. The graphics use the language of ideograms. The color range of the identity system consists of the three primitive colors of the brand: black, white, and red.

NEXT SPREAD
The identity system includes irreverent bears that are, according to Mariscal, "rascals, strange, not in the least bit sweet, who have fun, are up to no good, who have their own world, close to the fantasy world of children, are the star of the graphics."

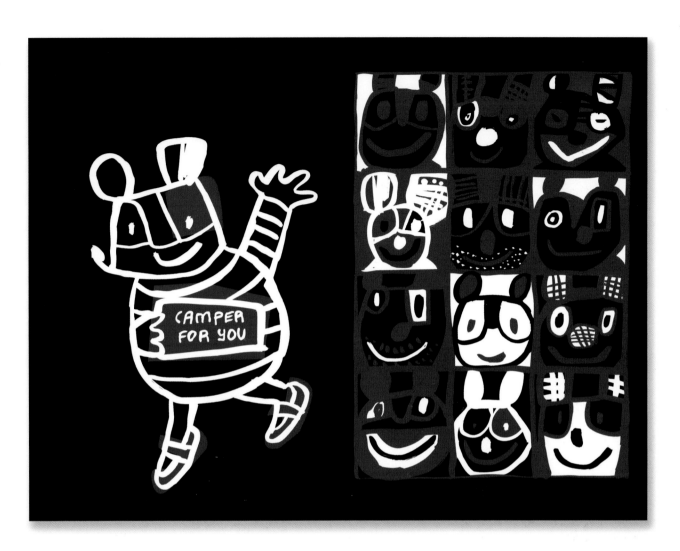

KEEP YOUR BEAT

CAMPER
FOR KIDS

ECOUTE LE SON DE TES CHAUSSURES

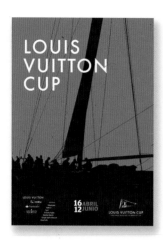

The identity for America's Cup is applied to corporate applications, merchandising elements, exterior image, as well as applications for advertising, and for the organization itself.

A series of posters use the hand-drawn logo for America's Cup with silhouetted images. These are accompanied with the identity system's bold color palette to communicate strength, power, and energy.

To transmit the characteristics of America's Cup, an avant-garde event, the applications, logo and posters use a free-form artistic treatment, for the typography as well as for the composition of the images and shapes.

Environmental graphics for the regattas in Valencia, Malmo-Shake, and Trapani, Spain, utilize all elements of the identity system. The clear and simple color choices maintain the presence of the visuals in a cluttered environment. The logo is never treated as a signature in a corner; it is always the primary communication.

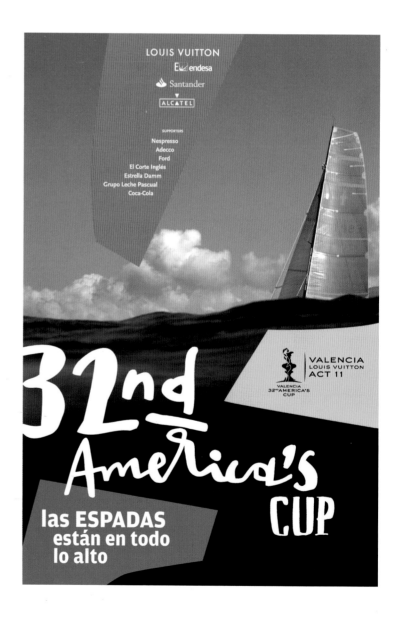

gamada is irrelevant, the primary symbol communicates so directly that any variation works. In the modern corporate world, Mariscal references the Nike swoosh. Even though Nike went through periods where it despised the swoosh, they continuously saw its value. An example of Mariscal's own work is the logo for Bancaja, a financial institution based in Spain. Since its launch, the asterisk symbol has displaced the word mark. The logo designed for Madrid's bid for the 2012 Olympics is another instance that the flame has become the memorable element.

For much of the twentieth century, logos were one or two color, simple, flat forms. In certain instances this resulted in some of history's most beautiful and successful marks. The CBS eye design by William Golden in 1951, the ABC logo designed by Paul Rand in 1962, and the Bell Company's logo designed by Saul Bass in 1969 each exemplify the grace and clarity in this approach. Although Mariscal agrees with the direction of creating simple rather than complex logos, he also believes a logo should fundamentally be expressive. He states, "Logos should be communicative, transmit a series of messages about the product, the activity, or the person it is representing. In order to get there, everything should be allowed." His approach lends to identity systems that function as well in one

color as multiple colors. This type of system provides the client with choices based on the final application.

Mariscal doesn't blame form as a common reason for a logo's failure. The final issue with failed logos is the inability to express the characteristics of the product or service they are intended to represent. Nevertheless, recognizing that certain logos may be beautiful and should be successful, examining the issue sometimes leads to unclear answers. "At times, it is a mystery why they don't work," says Mariscal.

Technology

In the past decade, multiple technologies and media have changed the ways we talk with the audience. Mariscal's attitude toward this ever-shifting aspect of the profession follows his usual pragmatic, yet optimistic philosophy. "Technology has changed our lives, our daily habits, our way of working, our tools," he explains. "New technology exists, and you can't turn your back on it. Of course, this has affected the final logo work." Before the digital revolution changed the design profession, Mariscal's work was done by hand. Today, the computer is the tool most often used to create the logos and systems. Response to the computer and its affect on design, and specifically logos, is almost entirely divided by generations. Designers who worked in a predigital period often

describe the issue as a change, perhaps not for the best, from a handmade craft and a more fluid way of thinking to a process that is more restrictive on the computer. Mariscal discusses the issue from the next generation, "Before the advent of the computer in design work, it was a complicated process. Now it is much simpler, faster, and more efficient." Whether this change in tools has affected his work is unclear. He acknowledges that everything is an influence, including new technology.

While Mariscal's logos have a sense of animation and fluidity, they succeed in the ability to maintain a clear and consistent communication across many applications. This is not accidental. He maintains a strong resolve to design logos that will be coherent in all applications. This demands many versions of a logo, from black and white to color, and in multiple configurations. He suggests, "Make chromatic variations, different sizes, versions that serve distinct functions, plan for any application." His logos are a tool kit with many pieces. They are taken apart, recombined, set in very different environments, and on many diverse applications. This modularity allows the logos to maintain a proprietary and consistent voice. Mariscal talks about the challenges of certain applications with his typical candidness. "All of the applications are important to me," he says. "When working

with logos and a visual identity, you don't leave things to chance." When presenting the logo for Madrid's 2012 Olympics bid, Mariscal applied the logo throughout Madrid onto transportation vehicles and signage. This allowed for a presentation depicting the reality of the logo's usage, and allowed the client to better understand the entire system.

The New

Mariscal's commitment to mentoring and educating younger designers is apparent in the atmosphere of Estudio Mariscal. When discussing logos and advice for other designers, Mariscal's enthusiasm for sharing information that helps others shines through. "Designers should do what they desire," he says. "They can be innovators and offer something new and unexpected, and make this world less boring. But they should be sincere. And most importantly, designers should not work just to become rich or famous. If that happens, let those things come on their own."

FROM TOP

Metropol Le Café
The logo for Metropol Cafe in Gran Hotel Domine Bilbao, Spain, refers to constructivist and art deco letterforms.

Zoo de Barcelona
Barcelona Zoo's logo uses amorphous shapes to suggest a paw print, animal shapes, and a face.

Swedish Socialist Party
The Swedish Socialist Party required a word mark and icon that reinforce the ideas of the handmade, and built.

Marmo Bar
The logo for the Marc Newson designed bar coordinates with the forms and design of the bar's environment.

Granship
Shizuoka Convention & Arts Center's logo ignored the expected approach of cold and dull forms to create a sense of excitement.

Benicàssim
Echoed shapes, the white crescents, curves of the letterforms, and circle are the elements that provide the Benicàssim logo with a cohesive quality.

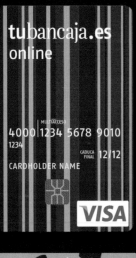

**Bancaja**
fondos

**Bancaja**
habitat

Bancaja
viajes

THIS SPREAD
Typically, financial institutions rely on a conservative color approach. Navy blue is a favorite, while red is sometimes not chosen for its association of being "in the red." The identity system for Bancaja relies on a vibrant multi hued palette to reinforce the ideas of the main components of communication: closeness to the client, and trust. The logo, symbol, and colors position the bank with an attitude of modernity.

The Bancaja symbol is derived from an asterisk, a symbol in the banking world that represents transparent communication. The symbol also refers to the meeting of two people with common interests.

Catàleg de Regals 2006

VÀLID FINS AL 31 DE MARÇ DE 2007

punts
Bancaja

Queremos prestarle la mejor atención

SERVICIO DE ATENCIÓN AL CLIENTE

PERDÓN

Bancaja

si no es bueno para ti, no es bueno para nosotros

La caja de todos y para todos

Bancaja

si no es bueno para ti, no es bueno para nosotros

Zero comissions, sense excepció.

Per a tots els clients particulars en les seues operacions domèstiques

0€

Bancaja

si no és bo per a tu, no és bo per a nosaltres

Queremos prestarle la mejor atención

SERVICIO DE ATENCIÓN AL CLIENTE

...!

Bancaja

si no es bueno para ti, no es bueno para nosotros

Abre tu vida a un nuevo entorno

GUIA INMOBILIARIA VERANO 2005

Bancaja
habitat

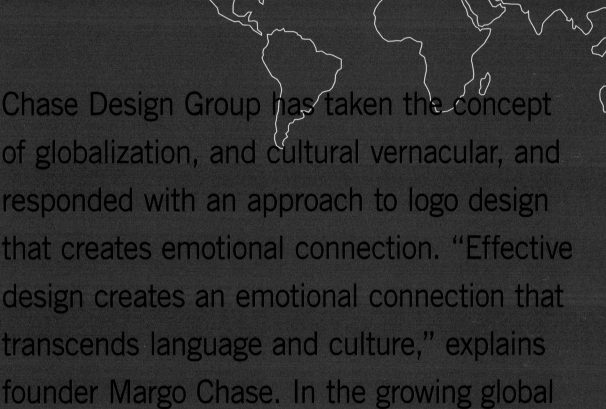

Chase Design Group, Los Angeles, California, U.S.A.

Chase Design Group has taken the concept of globalization, and cultural vernacular, and responded with an approach to logo design that creates emotional connection. "Effective design creates an emotional connection that transcends language and culture," explains founder Margo Chase. In the growing global market, this human connection is crucial to the success of any brand." Chase describes her approach as "brand-building."

OPPOSITE
The first step in the logo
and identity development for
the shoe company, Chinese
Laundry, was to identify
the core consumer. In this
instance, the consumer
is an upwardly mobile,
midtwenties, urban woman.

The creation of a logo is part of a process that includes brand strategy, identity development, packaging design, retail environments, advertising, and licensed product development. While emotional connection plays a primary role in the design process, Chase is pragmatically concerned with the client's needs and specifically the business challenges that need to be addressed.

Many of Chase's logos have an aesthetic and formal tone that implies careful consideration, high level of skill, and a remarkable and clear vision. The extreme attention to detail and visual forms in her logo design, however, are secondary to the considerations of a strategic direction. Chase's first step in the identity process is not to begin sketching, but to research, listen, and learn. "To translate a marketing brief into a great creative solution, we need a clear understanding of our client and the business challenge at hand," Chase explains. "We immerse ourselves in market research, strategic business plans, and trending data to provide a strong foundation." The competitive landscape informs her solutions. "We find additional insight by understanding how similar business challenges have been addressed in other industries," she says.

How individuals respond to the world is the core of Chase's trust in the power of emotional connection. This belief, that the responses of the audience are complex, is distilled clearly by Chase. "People are certain that they make decisions based on what they think (the *right* reason), but for the most part they make

decisions based on what they feel (the *real* reason)." This leads to the identification of an emotional target that will be central to the logo's communication. Every identity system is designed to evoke the desired response in the viewer: trust, excitement, fear, and so on.

Once the logo is designed and a system is approved, Chase attacks the applications with the same level of detail that is applied to the logo. "We love a great concept. What we love even more is bringing that concept to life in the world and watching it get results," she says. These results are a combination of the research, strategy, and logo applied with meticulous attention to a range of applications. "Every detail of a project is crucial, from the precise curve of a letterform to the texture of the paper that a logo is printed on," Chase explains.

Logos that are derivative and lack originality often fail to create a strong identity for a brand. Chase believes that the emotional connection is lost when a logo is not designed with the audience in mind. These can fail to resonate and be ignored. In addition to the messaging and communicative issues of poor logo design, pragmatic concerns are a priority for Chase, and they can cause failure in an identity system. "Very simply, logos that don't keep production limitations in mind fail when they reproduce badly," she says. These production limitations involve a lack of understanding of specific mediums, or poor execution that leads to poor reproduction.

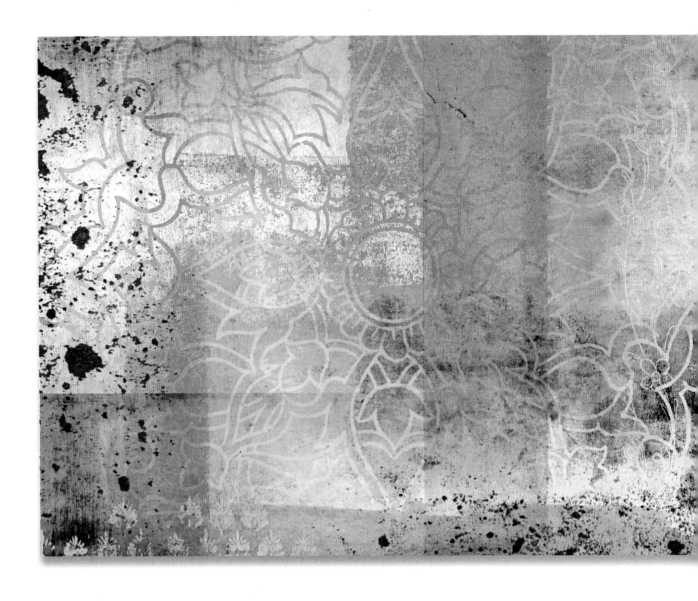

Lingerie Perdu is a retail
environment in Saudi Arabia.
The brand is targeted toward
the younger woman, often
educated abroad. The logo
turns to the Arabic tradition
of erotic poetry. The human
form is not allowed to be
used in the brand materials
or store environment. Hand
lettered phrases are built as
part of the identity system.
These reference the concept
of the "hidden," the desire
for all that is unseen.

LINGERIE *perdu*

NEXT SPREAD
The identity for Pearl
Dragon restaurant use
the preconceived symbols
and colors we associate
with "Chinese restaurant."
These elements are then
modified and given an
extra layer of style and
luxury. The red and gold
elements of the logo,
and materials used are
distressed and layered
communicating a sense
of age and depth.

PEARL DRAGON

THIS SPREAD
Kama Sutra is a diverse
line of erotic products.
Its mission is to produce
products that promote
healthy, open sexuality.
The logo, patterns, art,
color, and typography
work together to reinforce
this philosophy.

The use of traditional
Indian patterns, art,
and colors work to com-
municate an exotic, and
energetic feeling. In the
midst of this rich system,
the logo remains a clear
constant, maintaining
a proprietary position
in the market.

Since founding Chase Design Group in 1986,
Chase has been a pioneer in new media
and technologies. Her logos are designed to
go beyond print and packaging to interactive
formats used in digital applications for
broadcast and on the Web. Packaging,
however, remains a challenge. "The logo
is usually the easiest part," Chase says.
"Understanding enough about the production
process, materials, budget limitations,
and client expectations up front is crucial.
Overseas production can lead to strange
miscommunications and bad implementation
of the final design. We often have to hand
the design over to in-house production
departments so communicating intent and
establishing clear guidelines is critical and
can be very time-consuming." Chase enjoys
these challenges and continues to consider
packaging to be her favorite application.
"Good packaging requires an understanding
of the customer, the retail environment,
materials design, three-dimensional design,
as well as strong typography and image
design," she says.

The establishment of guidelines for the logo
usage is typically handled with a manual.
Training is also an essential part of Chase's
process to make a brand successful. The
creative partners, in-house and out, who are

responsible for implementing the logo must
understand how important it is for branding
to be consistent. She insists that these
creative partners should be given clear
guidelines and enough latitude to be creative.
The logo and identity system can be both
creative and successful.

The straightforward and pragmatic attitude
that is incorporated in Chase's philosophy
is misleading. This language of strategy and
business concerns would lead a reader to
believe that Chase's logos are conservative
and "safe" forms. The reality is that Chase's
personal vision and singular sense of direction
produce forms unlike any other designer.
These logos are surprising and unexpected.
Chase confirms her adherence to creative
solutions outside the typical way of thinking.
"There are lots of great logos out there, but
there is always room for something innovative
and beautiful," Chase says. "Everyone gets
started by imitating the things they love,
but great designers find a way to develop
unique work that makes the rest of us wish
we'd thought of it."

"People are certain that they make decisions based on what they think (the *right* reason), but for the most part they make decisions based on what they feel (the *real* reason)."

—Margo Chase, founder, Chase Design Group

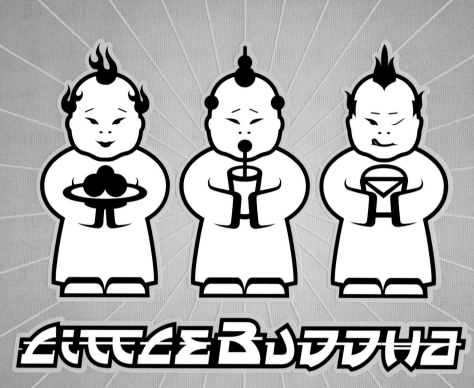

LITTLE BUDDHA

eat drink takeout

OPPOSITE
The highest quality of craft, paper, and production is a primary component of the identity system for Restaurant Marais. The logo is derived from baroque forms, updated and organic twist. Other elements, such as the edges of a baroque frame, and a subtle color palette communicate the feeling of the dining experience.

THIS PAGE
The identity for Little Buddha restaurant is designed with the elements and imagery often used in Asian-techno graphics. These elements, including the word mark, characters and gradations rely on our preconceived knowledge and impressions of this style. The younger, more immediate attitude is reflected in, not only the visual elements, but in the choice of merchandise for the logo's application.

CHICAIGAO

CROSBY ASSOCIATES

Bart Crosby
Chicago, Illinois, U.S.A.

TOP
From 1990 to the present, AIGA has experienced substantial growth. The logo for AIGA has historic brand equity. Rather than creating a completely different mark for AIGA Chicago, the updated system provides identity guidelines which assure visual consistency as a large number of varied independent designers create materials including print, environment, and screen-based applications.

BOTTOM
ColeTaylor is a leading, middle market bank with a mission to become the premier bank for Chicago area businesses and the people who own and manage them. The branding program includes a new identity system featuring a simplified name, a new symbol, and a new visual approach to all applications.

CAPTIVE RESOURCES

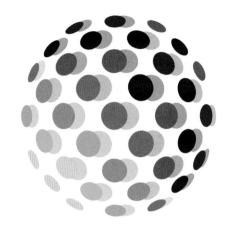

EimerStahl

SEARLE

CiU
DAD
Ciudad
CiUDAD
Ciudad

Michael Hodgson, Santa Monica, California, U.S.A.

Ph.D, Santa Monica, California, USA

Over the past ten years, branding has become a meaningless term. It has been co-opted, and its definition has been broadened to apply to anything from Coca-Cola to a description of an individual's quirks: "Betty's brand is her pink nail polish. She wears it every day." When discussing branding with Ph.D principal Michael Hodgson, the term "personality" peppers the conversation. Personality can be used in psychological terms to describe individual differences, or it can be used to construct a coherent and complete picture of a person.

OPPOSITE
Typically, an identity system consists of one logo, typeface, imagery, and color palette. Ciudad Restaurant has four logos. This choice reflects the multicultural menu taken from Latin countries around the world. The color palette reflects the attitude of these countries, and the logos use this palette in a free-form way.

The idea of personality applies to a person's behavior. Transferring this concept to an organization or product is a logical step for Hodgson. His logos also have a nod to humor and wit. This provides the identities with a more coherent and approachable voice.

Visual Personality

"I prefer to think of the work that we do as creating visual personalities, rather than the term branding, which has become part of the general public's everyday lexicon," Hodgson says. He follows this attention to the construction of a complete message in the design of each logo. Given the complexity of a company's personality, this would dictate elaborate formal solutions. Hodgson, however, bypasses this approach. "In a world where almost everything is designed, where there is, dare I say it, too much design, the last thing left is personality," Hodgson explains. The integration of a philosophy that presupposes an overdesigned environment drives Hodgson to create logos that maintain clarity and a Shaker-like plainness.

Once again, the idea of simplicity is an omnipresent term in the verbiage of a world-class identity designer. Hodgson's logos are simple and direct, but they are the foundation for flexible and layered visual systems. No solutions use a rigid unchanging system that allows for no derivation. Each system is built to support the logo, but allow the designer to create a varied range of materials that remain similar in tone, without being slavishly consistent. "Our systems are usually flexible,"

he maintains. "We stay away from simply applying the logo to each item of stationery in the same way. This raises challenges for us but always results in a much stronger personality."

The directness of Hodgson's approach applies to symbols and words. While some of his logos use a symbol, they all are grounded with a straightforward treatment of the name. "Obviously a word mark is great because it immediately tells you the name of the company," he says. "But a symbol can transcend that, taking it to the point where you immediately know who or what it is, even if you're reading a foreign language." For example, the Apple symbol or Nike swoosh have strong proprietary value based on their continued usage for decades. "A symbol takes longer to establish, and often only happens after the symbol has spent some time being seen together with the word mark," Hodgson explains.

Flexibility

Hodgson's idea of personality constructs a coherent and complete picture of a product. The entirety of that personality is communicated through applications. The system's flexibility, therefore, is at the core of the success or failure of a logo. "Logos fail because mindless applications are produced, often based on manuals that don't allow for flexibility," says Hodgson. While each designer can cite his or her favorite application to design, Hodgson redirects the priority. "The most important, and for me, favorite application depend on the client." His logo and system for Foundation Press relied on their fleet of trucks and delivery

THIS SPREAD
John Ford directed some of the most mythic and memorable films of the 20th century including *Stagecoach, How the West Was Won*, and *The Searchers*. *Ford at Fox*, the 164 page coffee table book celebrates his career. The logo is applied to a variety of applications such as the book, CDs, and posters. The form reflects Ford's straightforward and masculine approach.

The poster uses the bold color palette: red, black, and white, and typography that echoes the forms of the logo. The imagery is a critical component of the communication, and the identity system is built to incorporate this.

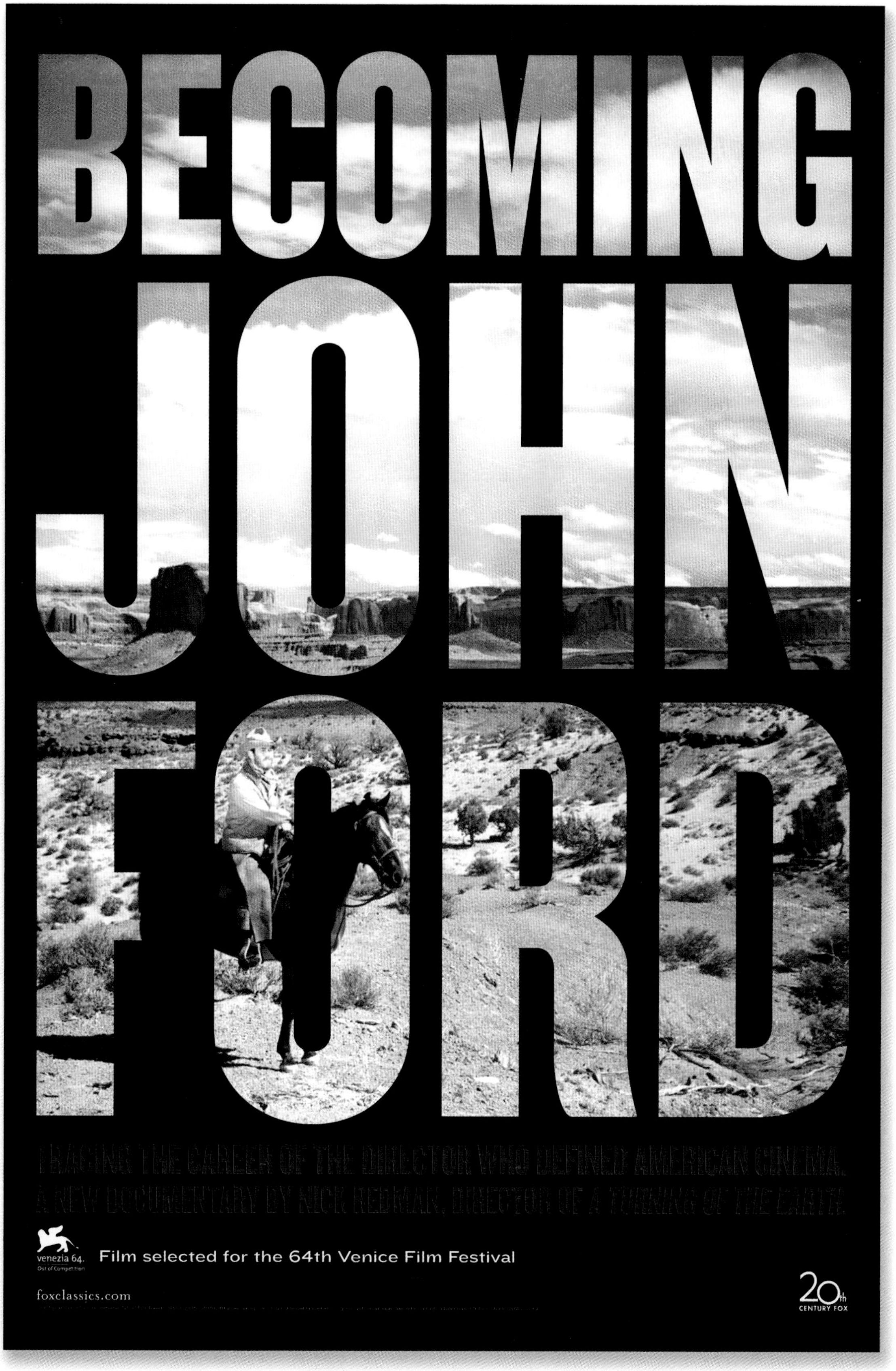

BECOMING JOHN FORD

TRACING THE CAREER OF THE DIRECTOR WHO DEFINED AMERICAN CINEMA.
A NEW DOCUMENTARY BY NICK REDMAN, DIRECTOR OF A TURNING OF THE EARTH.

venezia 64.
Out of Competition

Film selected for the 64th Venice Film Festival

foxclassics.com

20th
CENTURY FOX

Bergamot Cafe is in Bergamot Station, Southern California's largest art gallery complex and cultural center. It's located on eight acres in the heart of Santa Monica featuring contemporary art galleries, The Santa Monica Museum of Art, architecture and design firms, and a frame shop. The logo focuses on the varied individuals at the cafe, as opposed to the food or environment.

The identity system, with an illustrative icon, and geometric word mark, is the foundation for a visual system. The system includes, not only logo, color, and typography, but specific applications, such as T-shirts, and an overall tonality. This is possible as Ph.D maintains control of the identity system and its use.

vehicles as primary communicators. "These were most successful (and therefore most critical) applications and have become their most effective form of advertising," Hodgson says.

In one instance, the range of applications that Hodgson addresses has extended beyond stationery and vehicles. "I designed *Appetite for Destruction*, the first Guns N' Roses album, which established a strong identity for them," he explains. "We used a cross design on it, and one of the band members loved it and had it tattooed on his arm." His system for David Fincher's company, No. 13, includes the standard stationery items, but he also designed the room numbers and the numbers for the parking lot.

The simple yet playful attitude of Hodgson's logos would point to a specific and limited palette of inspiration. Rather than citing the Shakers or Mies van der Rohe solely, he discusses a wide range of inspirational sources. "For inspiration, I don't look at design annuals," he says. "I go to museums, look at books on art, and architecture. I look at flowers and go to the movies. As the name of Paul Smith's book suggests, you can find inspiration anywhere."

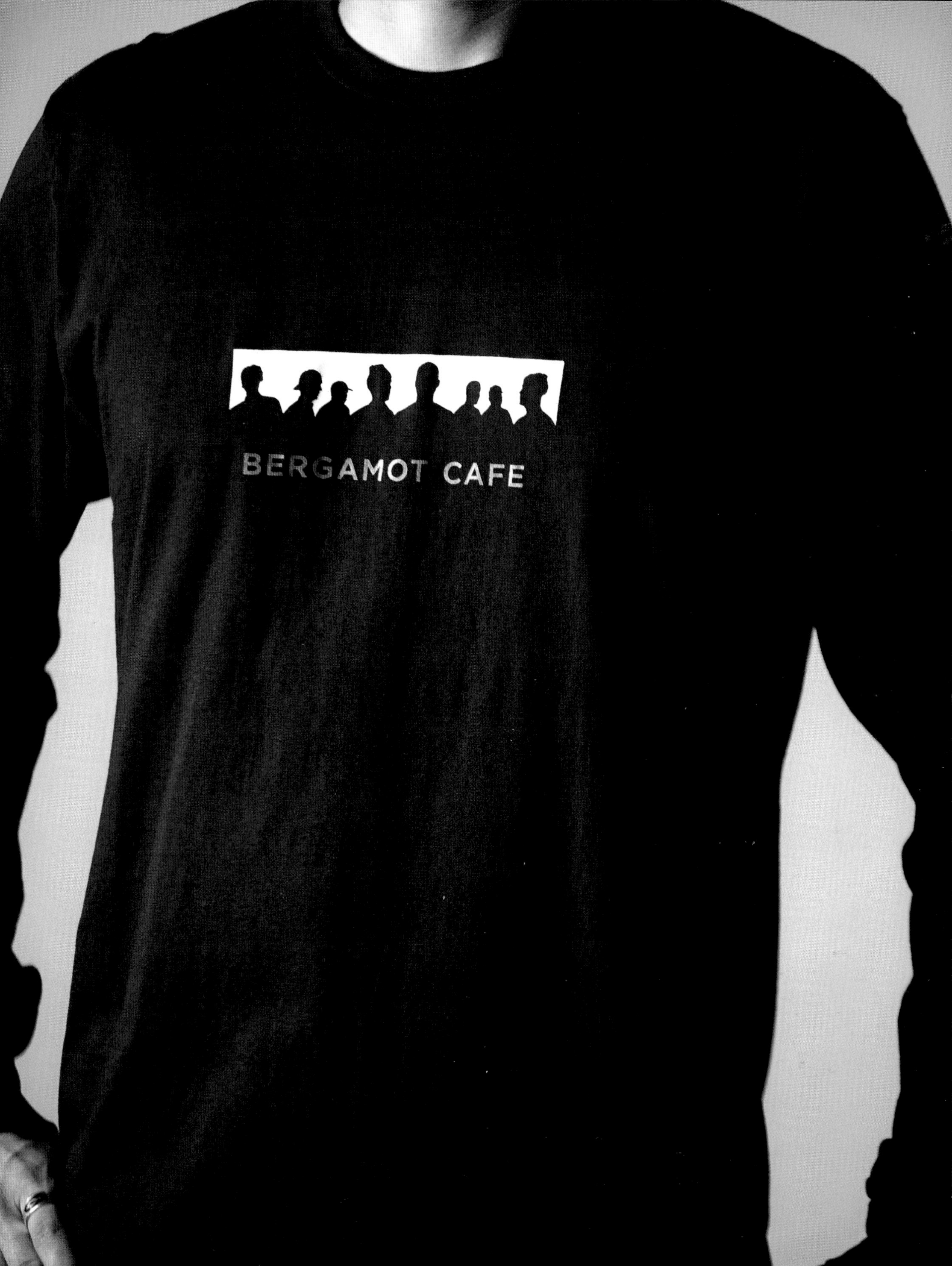
BERGAMOT CAFE

Border Grill

Border Grill

1445 4TH. Street, Santa Monica, CA 90401, (310) 451-1658

ME LLAMO
-Josh McKinney-
sous chef, las vegas
[702] 632 7403

Border Grill

Santa Monica

**1445 4th street
santa monica, ca 90401
(310) 451 1655
(310) 394 2049 fax**

mandalay bay resort & casino
3950 las vegas blvd south
las vegas, nv 88119
(702) 632 7403
(702) 632 6915 fax

www.bordergrill.com

Mary Sue Milliken
Chef / Owner
Border Grill - Ciudad

310 453 8411
marysue@bordergrill.com

THIS SPREAD
Border Grill is an upscale,
modern Mexican restaurant
with a vibrant setting.
Chefs Mary Sue Milliken and
Susan Feniger present bold
foods and flavors, making
Border Grill the new standard
for gourmet Mexican fare
in Los Angeles. The original
identity was designed by
noted designer, Mike Fink.
All illustrations and hand
lettering are by Huntley/Muir.
Hodgson updated and
clarified the original identity
and reverted back to its
original black and white
color scheme. The system
relies on the handmade
in almost every instance,
from the word mark to the
illustrations. This communicates a sense of spontaneity
and excitement. It also
represents the casual, but
sophisticated atmosphere.

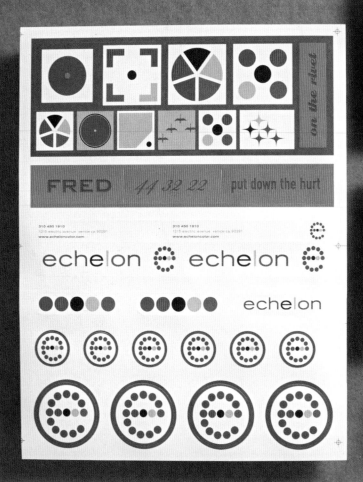

ABOVE
Echelon is a color and
retouching house, owned
by two individuals with
a passion for cycling.
The identity is based
upon the idea of dots,
the core of their business.

The dots and the five colors
incorporate the interests
of the owners. The colors
are the world cycling
championship colors and
the *e* is round, reminiscent
of a bike wheel.

"Never show the client anything you don't love."

—**Michael Hodgson, principal, Ph.D**

ABOVE
The equity of the logo for the hotel, No.13, is built from the recognition of the mark in variable environments. The actual numeral may change, but each application reinforces the identity with consistent shapes, elements, materials, and colors. The purely typographic solution is based on Didot, the first modern typeface designed by Firmin Didot in 1784.

Matteo Bologna, New York, New York, U.S.A.

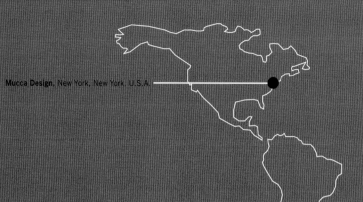

Mucca Design, New York, New York, U.S.A.

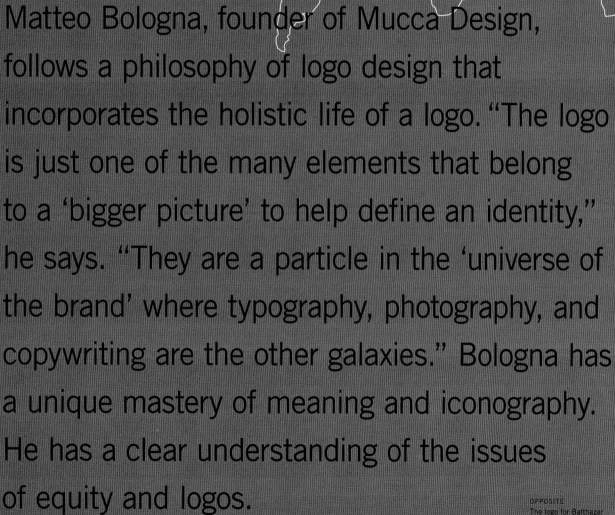

Matteo Bologna, founder of Mucca Design, follows a philosophy of logo design that incorporates the holistic life of a logo. "The logo is just one of the many elements that belong to a 'bigger picture' to help define an identity," he says. "They are a particle in the 'universe of the brand' where typography, photography, and copywriting are the other galaxies." Bologna has a unique mastery of meaning and iconography. He has a clear understanding of the issues of equity and logos.

OPPOSITE
The logo for Balthazar Restaurant defines the traditional feel of the restaurant with freshness and an attention to period detail. Applications range from signage, and stationery, to cookbooks.

Custom typeface design is very challenging because it is laborious and time-consuming, but contrary to logo design, it is the one that is easier to get approved."

—Matteo Bologna, founder, Mucca Design

OPPOSITE
An upper east side luxury food market since 1915, Butterfield Market is recognized for superior quality. A master brand creates a clear visual statement, and allows the brand to expand into other businesses and regions, while maintaining a strong and proprietary presence.

TOP LEFT
Functioning like a walking billboard, the shopping bag for Butterfield Market incorporates pictorial elements and patterns. The unique color palette and flexible typography provide ease of recognition.

TOP RIGHT
The identity system for Balthazar Restaurant, and its multiple businesses demonstrates the strength of a holistic approach. Rather than relying on a simple and flat icon used repeatedly, each application of the logo is unique. The commonality is created with elements such as color, logo, and typography. The overall tone of the visuals, however, provide the greatest amount of equity.

Inherently, a logo has no meaning. It is only when placed in the context of other messages that it adopts meaning. "The logo acquires its meaning from the other elements and not vice versa," he explains. "The Apple mark is just the drawing of an apple. This means nothing by itself, but when placed within the context of the company's philosophy, products, and communications, it acquires value and enormous equity." Bologna wryly states that the best way to design a successful logo is "to design a logo for a company that will be successful, and by consequence, your logo will be considered as such."

"Simple" is the standard answer for a world-class designer when asked whether a logo should be complex or minimal. This is Bologna's answer as well. But he quickly contradicts himself. "After designing logos for more than twenty years, the simpler the better. But, unfortunately, we never follow this rule," he says. "Recently, we designed a system for a restaurant (Country) with more than thirty variations of the logotype." This solution is possible when a client is remarkably focused visually, or if the initial creator of the logo is the designer controlling all aspects of the system. In this case, Country only retains

Mucca Design for all of its design services. "I am able to maintain consistency by making sure that the same designer is always monitoring the project, even after it is finished," Bologna explains. He uses this metaphor to describe the alternative: "If they were being serviced by different designers, this would be a recipe for disaster."

Mucca Typo is a division of Mucca Design, dedicated to the creation of fonts. The level of obsessive precision necessary to design a typeface migrates to Bologna's logo and identity work. The choice between symbols and word marks is deflected by Bologna with a discussion about the Coca-Cola letterforms. "The Coca-Cola logo is one of the examples of how good quality in typography is not necessary," Bologna says. "The original word mark was a terrible script that haunted poor designers who had to redesign it every ten to fifteen years. But everybody remembers it, so we can consider it successful as a logo." Alternatively, the word mark for Nike is not memorable to Bologna. In this instance, the swoosh is the mnemonic property. Both logos have equity and an ingrained philosophy of values. These values have been married to both the Coca-Cola word mark and the Nike swoosh by consistent control of the logo and context.

Misrepresentation

Direct communication is not an issue for Bologna. "Identities that fail are the ones where the owner is an idiot, or where there are too many people who make decisions," he says. This statement is a summation of the common problem of misrepresentation. "Most of the time, failed identities come from companies that lie to their customers," Bologna continues. "Unfortunately this becomes the designer's problem." A good logo can never save a bad product. The designer's role is to focus and visually impart the values and messages of a client. If the client misrepresents a company's product or values, the logo can never succeed. The logo is a promise. If that promise is not kept, the customer will feel betrayed, and the logo will lose all credibility.

Bologna's logos vary from simple one-color solutions, such as the Rizzoli *R*, to complex multilayered logos, such as the Adobe Design Achievement Awards logo. "Some of the old rules of using no more than two colors or not using gradients in a logo/mark are passé in a period when you can design on continuous tones for printers or for the web," he explains. Bologna's identity systems have a quality of flexibility that is more connected to industrial revolution technologies than digital reproduction. The logos for restaurants, particularly Pastis, are designed to give the impression of history. The logo has slightly different variations to convey the sense that it has evolved over time. The multiple versions also respond to the medium used. These versions include logos that look rubber-stamped, reproduced with old lithographic techniques, or hand-made applications.

Thematic Variations

Bologna uses historical idioms to communicate a company's character. This solution is often used on logos designed for restaurants and hospitality clients who are more interested in producing an overall gestalt, or atmosphere, than communicating a hard-core set of corporate values. The logo operates as an identifier and as a prop for the theatrical experience of dining in a restaurant. The historical forms rely on the customer's knowledge and recognition, linking them to a specific time or place. The power of these logos is derived from their narrative connection. The viewer connects the visual forms and applications to his or her own internal stories. The addition of a sense of reassurance adds to the success of Bologna's logos. The applications are the vehicles for the success.

ABOVE
Country is a Manhattan restaurant that serves contemporary and sophisticated dishes featuring locally grown organic ingredients. The interior design of the restaurant is a mix of eclectic details and midcentury modern. The logo, a monogram of a *C*, is a set of randomly mixed letterforms in multiple hues. This conveys the warm and playful tone of the restaurant's character.

OPPOSITE
The identity for Gracious Gourmet takes its cue from the product. The line of gourmet chutneys, glazes, and spreads utilizes a strong visual brand that communicates the company's commitment to high quality ingredients, exciting flavors, and ease of use.

Classical botanical prints are combined with a rich color palette and modern sans serif typeface for the Gracious Gourmet. The mix of classic images, unexpected colors, and clear typographic language communicates the company's commitment to quality, and a fresh approach to cooking.

mango
pineapple
chutney

the gracious gourmet

fig
almond
spread

mild
barbeque

Net Wt 11 oz (315 g)

Wekselbaum
ox 218, Bridgewater, CT 06752
0.350.1213 F 860.350.1214
yw@thegraciousgourmet.com

the gracious gourmet

Nancy Wekselbaum
P.O. Box 218, Bridgewater, CT 06752
T 860.350.1213 F 860.350.1214
nancyw@thegraciousgourmet.com

the gracious gourmet

Nancy Wekselbaum
P.O. Box 218, Bridge
T 860.350.1213 F
nancyw@thegracio

The Presidio Social Club is set in an old military barracks in San Francisco's historic military base, the Presidio. The logo incorporates the building's address to help the guests find the restaurant in a group of nondescript barracks.

The menus for Presidio Social Club convey a fictional history, complete with old photos and vintage illustrations. This links the Presidio Social Club restaurant to the area's heritage. The custom typefaces of the identity system are taken from the Victorian language of the Barbary Coast and, according to Bologna, "many John Wayne movies."

One of Milan's most famous upscale restaurant brands, Saint Ambroeus takes its name from Milan's patron saint. The logo for the flagship restaurant on Manhattan's Madison Avenue repositions the restaurant's identity to convey its many personalities, from a morning espresso bar to a sophisticated late night restaurant. The custom typefaces and cloud motif relate to the brand's origin, but refresh and modernize its communication.

The logo is incorporated into a line of packaging for the restaurant's products. The colors and custom typefaces are supplemented with texture and a sense of history. These extra emotionally connected elements give the brand visual joy.

RIGHT
In order to create a unified design theme for Schiller's Liquor Bar on Manhattan's lower east side, the logo is based on authentic details of the neighborhood. The letterforms were created by a specialized calligrapher. A custom typeface simulates handwriting with oddly sized, and unevenly spaced letters.

BOTTOM
Simplifying the wine buying experience, Schiller's wine bottles plainly display the quality. This element does not use the logo, but the attitude communicates a casual lightness contributing to the entire brand experience and concept.

RIGHT
BUR is a division of
Italian publishing giant
RCS. The logo is a redesign
of a preexisting 1970s era
logo. The new logo and
accompanying attitude for
the book design combine
the company's history
with a modern approach.

BELOW
The logo for one of the
world's premier publishing
brands, Rizzoli, exists on a
wide variety of applications.
The logo stands clearly
with a neutral attitude that
allows for many types of
content. The hand drawn
R maintains a clear identity
communicating classic
excellence, and modernity.

Felix Beltran & Asociados, Mexico City, Hidalgo, Mexico

Felix Beltran was born in Havana, Cuba, trained as a designer in the United States and France, designed for the Communist Party of Cuba, and later moved to Mexico, becoming a Mexican citizen. This varied life has led to the design of some of the world's most exuberant and powerful posters. Beltran's logo work is no less powerful, but it has a remarkable clarity and rigor. Ideas such as "work hard, functional, and again, work hard" pepper Beltran's discussions on logos and identity.

OPPOSITE
The logo for Estamex, a company that manufactures modular panels for office spaces, represents Beltran's minimal and clear voice. Used as a repeat pattern, the logo maintains integrity, reinforces the product, and energizes.

"Work, work, and work."

—Felix Beltran, founder, Felix Beltran & Asociados

Minimalism

Architects Luis Barragán, John Pawson, and Tadao Ando have a commonality of reductive forms in their work. Beltran uses the same minimal approach to logos. "For me, all design should be functional, where nothing is out of its role," Beltran states. "Every element should be derived from the project's content and needs." His logos universally take the exacting approach of reducing the subject to its necessary elements. No superfluous forms are incorporated. This leads to a vision that creates memorable and sharply defined communications. Almost all designers who excel in the field of identity agree on the need for simplicity in logo design. Beltran, however, escalates this rule. His logos support ideas first introduced by Russian Constructivists who proclaimed that distillation of form was required to create a universal language that the masses could understand.

"Simple logos are easier to perceive than complex logos," Beltran says. But he adds to this common theme that "we may equate simple with something missing. On the contrary, the lack of surplus—what is not there—creates the power of a logo." His approach to color in logo design follows similar reductive thinking. Beltran's logos typically are monochromatic, relying on the strength and association of one strong color association. For example, the tone used for the Grapus–Diseño Grafico logo is neither yellow or orange. The ochre tone

is specific and proprietary, using color in the same manner as Tiffany blue. The color is given more prominence with the lack of a complex color palette for the accompanying identity system.

A common theme in Beltran's logos is the use of an initial letter converted into a geometric symbol. He designed his first logo with the letter *v v* to evoke the front of the building and its balconies. "A name is comprised of sounds," Beltran says. "These are converted into letters and then into a symbol." This correlates with the theory that a word or symbol seen and heard at the same time has stronger memory associations. Coupled with the rigorous minimalism, this philosophy creates powerful and memorable symbols that once recognized, become closely tied to the client.

Tools

At the beginning of Beltran's career, the primary tools were T squares, triangles, ruling pens, and Plaka gouache paint. He has used evolving technology not to change his vision, but to allow for more options. "For me, the computer is a tool that facilitates broad experimentation and exploration," Beltran explains. "This was not possible previously." While the final logos may seem effortless and simple, the amount of rigorous attention to detail and refinement are the ingredients to their success. The negative shapes of the logos are as refined as the positive forms. Angles are carefully considered and echoed. Forms may appear to be easily drawn with the circle tool

OPPOSITE
The stationery system for the Estamex identity remains true to the original intent. No extraneous detail is added, the typography is consistent with one size and weight, and the placement remains consistent on each piece of the system. The logo is the primary focus with no distractions.

NEXT SPREAD
Hospitalaria Coyoacán is a hospital with four branches. The logo, a simple group of four squares represents this idea in the simplest and most elegant of forms. The back of the stationery uses this logo in a repeat pattern. The strength of this solution is the clarity of the solution.

The backside of the letterhead for Hill Printing incorporates a pattern based on the logo. The shapes refer to the letter *H* and printing processes.

Estamex
Rosario 245
Col Valle Dorado
Tlanepantla
Edo de México 03300
53789583
53789776

Estamex
Rosario 245
Col Valle Dorado
Tlanepantla
Edo de México 03300
53789583
53789776

Alberto Zuñiga
Director

Estamex
Rosario 245
Col Valle Dorado
Tlanepantla
Edo de México 03300
53789583
53789776

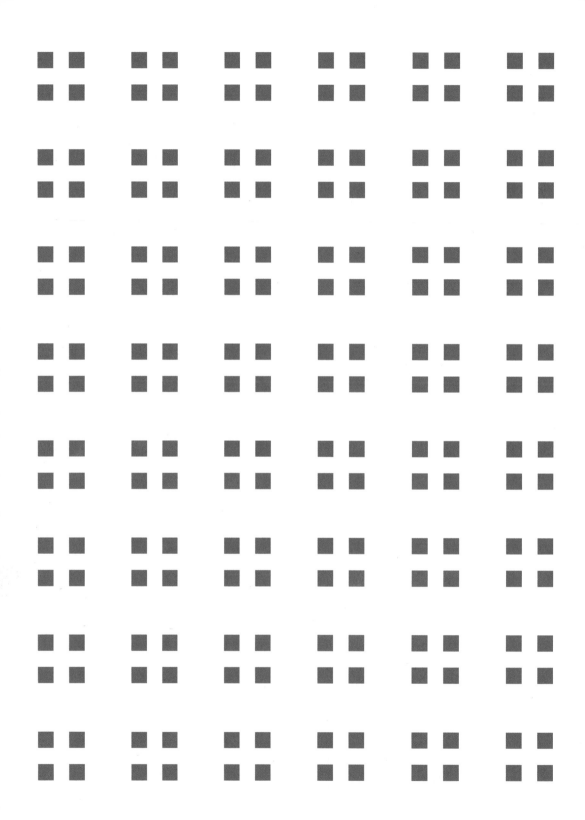

Hill
Villahermosa 186
Col Portales
México DF 03300
56889488

José Aguilera
Director

THIS SPREAD
Following Beltran's
minimal aesthetic, the
business card for Hill
Printing reduces the
elements of the system
to their most basic forms:
one typeface and the
H shape logo.

NEXT SPREAD
The Steelmex logo is
a reinterpretation of
the client's product,
metal panel systems
for offices and industry,
and the shape of the *S*.
This is a combination
of a monogram and icon.

The logo for Grapus,
a design office takes
one of design's most
elemental forms, a circle,
and alters its location
to become the monogram
of the initial, *G*.

in Adobe Illustrator, but they are handmade and complex in creation. This exacting attention to detail gives the logos a level of clarity and grace that would be easily mishandled without Beltran's touch.

Beltran addresses new technologies with a minimal answer that relates to his visual approach. "The logo and its applications should be appreciated in all media," he says The austerity of Beltran's logos facilitate this appreciation across various media. The accompanying visual systems follow a reductive approach that enhances the logo. The typeface chosen on many systems is Univers, which was designed by Adrian Frutiger in 1956, following many of the same minimalist ideas as Beltran's work. The size and weight of the type is consistent, and the color palette is often one tone of gray. This lack of additional elements places all emphasis on the logo, enhancing its prominence.

While some designers promote the importance and success of identity manuals, Beltran is less optimistic. His experience with standards manuals is that they are often not used. "I have found that the identity manual is often not instrumental," Beltran says. "This creates incoherence in the logo's applications." The addition of multiple users of a logo adds to the confused results. While maintaining integrity of a logo is difficult with one end user, the easy transmission of files and art creates a multitude of possible logo use violations. Beltran combats this loss of equity with the straightforward approach of the logo design. The extremely simple forms are more difficult

to mishandle, and the inflexible visual systems give less creative license to the end user. This maintains integrity of the logo.

Many designers cite their favorite logo applications as the most unique, such as vehicles, uniforms, and dinnerware. Beltran, however, prefers the primary applications. "I enjoy the most basic," he says. "These are the most difficult, such as the stationery where the mark can use up too much space, the envelope where the space is insufficient for stamps, or the business card that has too much text." Beltran's continuous refinement and attention to detail solve these problems. These are often the most visible applications and give the logo a strong position to create equity and value.

"Everything should be functional" is Beltran's mantra. But functional is not enough, "The present time encourages rushing," Beltran says. "Frequently we look for results that are both fast and easy, and this affects the work." The first casualty in this fast-paced race is the clarity of the client's objectives. Beltran's approach demands a commitment and understanding of these objectives. "When the needs and objectives of a project are not clear, the logo and applications can never be clear either," he says. The success of Beltran's logos relies on the ability to penetrate the content, objectives, and functional requirements. His adherence to rigor is the quality that moves the identities past successful and into remarkable. "Work, work, and work," Beltran advises.

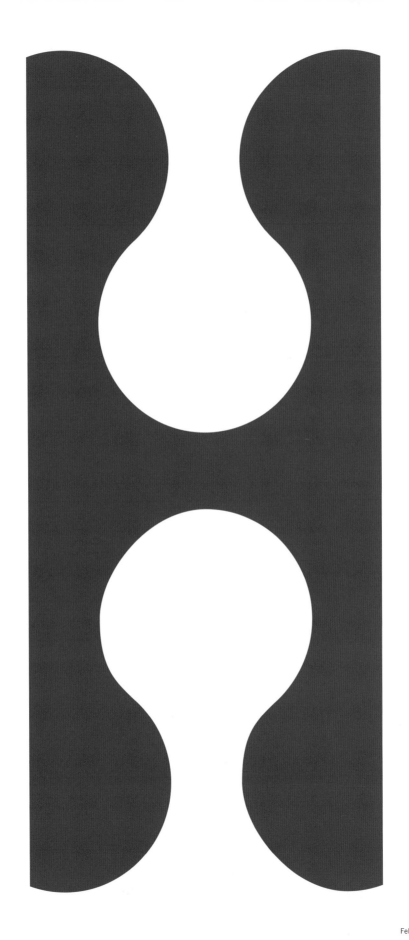

LISKA + ASSOCIATES

Steven Liska
Chicago, Illinois, U.S.A.

ABOVE
Expand Beyond is one of the
worldwide leaders in mobile
software for IT and application
management. The logo expresses
the wireless component of the
company's product. The forms
of the logo are friendly and
approachable. In the instance
of a complex and ever-changing
technology, this communication
is necessary. These forms are
echoed in the architecture
of the trade show environment.

THEATRE GOODMAN
ON STAGE

Vol. 20, No. 3

Mary Zimmerman's *Pericles*
World Premiere *Mariela in the Desert*
Getting the Scoop on *The Story*

THEATRE
GOODMAN
CHAIRMAN'S COUNCIL

THEATRE
GOODMAN
PREMIER SOCIETY

THEATRE
GOODMAN
WOMEN'S BOARD

THEATRE
GOODMAN

Advice for Successful Logo Design

Unless you're designing for a fashion company, design isn't fashion. Understand the brand essence, audiences, and symbolism first. Then move away from your comfort zone and explore solutions rooted in the project's goals and objectives. Remember, the essence of the brand experience needs to be communicated.

ABOVE
Three guiding principles, quality, diversity, and community, are at the center of Goodman Theatre's mission to be the premier cultural organization in Chicago. The theater provides productions and programs that make an essential contribution to the quality of life. The logo is designed to communicate the robust and energetic aspects of the institution. The system incorporates different brand extensions for existing programs, and others yet to be created.

stay.

a modern dog hotel

Where dogs enjoy exceptional facilities, premium services, attentive staff and a beautiful setting on the river.

BNSF^{SM}

RAILWAY

TOP
Stay. is a modern dog hotel where dogs enjoy exceptional facilities, premium services, attentive staff, and a beautiful setting. The logo builds our experience of a happy dog, the wagging tail. The logo uses different breeds and types of dogs. The common factor is the green box and tail graphic.

BOTTOM
Ten years after forming from a merger, BNSF required a new visual brand that would reflect its current presence as a unified company. Based on audience research, a complete branding program now exists including fleet graphics, stationery, uniforms, and signage.

TIM BIEBER: DIRECTOR, CINEMATOGRAPHER

REEL INFO
ARCHIVE FTP

CURRENT REEL

CH1CAGO
VISIONS

25
YEARS
SUNDANCE
INSTITUTE

SUNDANCE
INSTITUTE™

DISCOVERING AND **DEVELOPING INDEPENDENT ARTISTS** AND **AUDIENCES**

FILM FESTIVAL
FEATURE FILM
DOCUMENTARY
FILM MUSIC
THEATRE

ADAMSMORIOKA, INC.

Sean Adams
Beverly Hills, California, U.S.A.

AdamsMorioka, Inc., Beverly Hills, California, U.S.A.

My partner, Noreen Morioka, and I have been called the new Ray and Charles Eames, the new Donny and Marie, and the Paris Hiltons of Design. Comparisons aside, we lead a team working in multiple media creating vibrant, clear, and at times, humorous identities since 1994. While the logo and identity systems created are appropriate and unique to each client, the overall theme of our logo work reflects the attitude of our location in Southern California.

OPPOSITE
A simple word mark and "glow" are the basic elements of the Sundance Institute identity. The glow represents the sun, energy, light, and film. The custom letterforms are modern, but refer to Sundance's western heritage, as in the horseshoe *U*.

FILM FESTIVAL
FEATURE FILM
DOCUMENTARY
FILM MUSIC
THEATRE

1000 Wilshire Boulevard, 1st Floor
Beverly Hills, California 90001
www.sundance.org

DISCOVERING and DEVELOPING INDEPENDENT ARTISTS and AUDIENCES

SUNDANCE
INSTITUTE

John Smith
Assistant, Sundance Film Festival

1000 Wilshire Boulevard, 1st Floor
Beverly Hills, California 90001

PHN 310.345.6789
FAX 310.345.6780
jsmith@sundance.org
www.sundance.org

SUNDANCE
INSTITUTE

FILM FESTIVAL
FEATURE FILM
DOCUMENTARY
FILM MUSIC
THEATRE

SUNDANCE
INSTITUTE

○ FILM FESTIVAL
○ FEATURE FILM
○ DOCUMENTARY
○ FILM MUSIC
○ THEATRE

SUNDANCE | FEATURE FILM
INSTITUTE

SUNDANCE
FILM FESTIVAL

SUNDANCE
INSTITUTE

The visual elements are often bright and colorful, the attitude is playful, and the communication is clear and direct. The identity solutions follow a clear set of processes and rules, but the final result is often defined by the system's ability to evolve and change.

The First Time

One of our first identity projects was for the Pacific Design Center, one of the western United States' largest interior design centers. The client asked for a mark that could have four languages of the Pacific Rim at the same time. The final product was a logo system that functioned like a weaving or textile made of the multiple languages. This was our first accidental step into a solution that inspired creativity, rather than constraining the process. Since then, most of the logos we've designed, or the systems that are built around the logos, reflect this ethic.

Complex Thinking

Within the color and playful attitude, one of the most important roles of the logo is to identify the client, rather than to describe its business or product. For example, a wirehaired fox terrier drinking coffee while sitting on a teacup will never be found within our work. The logo is meant to identify, like a person's name. It doesn't tell me what you do, or what you like to eat, but I know who you are. Simple and direct forms best achieve this. A strong proponent for simplicity, I strive for longevity, transcending current styles or

trends, and focus on communication. Because shape and color are two of the most important ways to achieve mnemonic value, I use simple forms and clear colors to reach this goal. Our logos also typically ask a question. The Oxygen logo, for example, poses the question to the viewer, "Why does it read 'oh!?'" While it is a simple question, it is enough to engage the viewer and create a more memorable response.

Human beings have been making symbols to represent things, ideas, people, and places for multiple millennia. This makes symbols extremely effective tools. Unfortunately, life today is drastically more complex than life in the Greek classical age. We are bombarded by images continuously. From every corporation to the local plumber, the idea of a corporate symbol has been universally adopted. There are simply too many symbols in the marketplace for a symbol alone to do its job. Word marks make the communication clearer and stronger. This makes the letterforms and name even more critical.

It's easy to forget that we rarely, if ever, see a logo in a void. Yet logos are often presented to the client on letter-sized boards on white backgrounds. This can be misleading because a logo will always be seen in the context of other messages in the physical world. When presenting to the client, I use the logo on typical applications such as a business card and stationery system, signage, or television screen to show the logo in context. Complex logos have never

My First Logo
My first logo was designed for Apple computers' in-house newsletter when I was fifteen. My father was a program designer in San Francisco and told me some friends of his at a new company needed a masthead for their newsletter, which would be photocopied and stapled together. I hand drew a terrible apple made up of a series of horizontal rules. This was before Saul Bass, one of the world's best logo designers, designed a similar logo for AT&T, so I assume Saul copied me.

THIS SPREAD
As a fast growing and expanding company, Wasserman Media Group's identity is designed to represent the activity and energy of the company. The identity system also allows for brand extensions and new divisions. As the primary home for the logo is on air, and in a Web environment, the icon is designed to animate and use a wide spectrum of colors. A one-color version of the logo exists, but is almost never used.

The stationery system is printed on both sides. The logo is scaled to occupy the entire backside of the letterhead. This reinforces the power and mnemonic value of the icon, and communicates WMG's commitment to many forms of entertainment and sports.

PMS 3265 PMS 3975 PMS 331 PMS 386

Kids like colors that are raw and
energized. We use combinations that
are unexpected, the more obnoxious,
the better.

KIT 2 — SHAPES

These are the shapes that are used as backgrounds,
windows or any other graphic element. They are
purposefully abstract. We don't want shapes that
make icons, like a cake or a car.

KIT 3 — PATTERNS

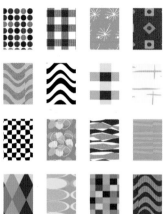

Disney ClubHouse Disney patterns

These are Disney patterns, Minnie's skirt, Cinderella
sparkles, Tomorrowland rockets, and ClubHouse
letterforms. Use at least one of these on all items.
This is that dash of magic. This lets our audience
know that Disney is talking to them. Don't add any
more to this collection. We want our audience to
get to know these as Disney ClubHouse patterns

Disney ClubHouse exterior patterns

These are exterior patterns, wood, brick, astroturf.
All of our patterns are made with colors from our
color palette. Don't add any more to this collection.
We want our audience to get to know these as
Disney ClubHouse patterns

KIT 5 — DISNEY PATTERNS

KIT 4 — EXTERIOR PATTERNS

ABCDEFGHIJKLMN
OPQRSTUVWXYZ
abcdefghijklmn
opqrstuvwxyz
1234567890?!~""{}

This is the Italic version of the ClubHouse Serif.
It's another alternative to be used for supportive
and secondary information, like "Happy Birthday"
on a birthday card invitation.

ClubHouse Gothic light
ABCDEFGHIJKLMNOPQRSTUVWXYZ
abcdefghijklmnopqrstuvwxyz
1234567890?!~""{}

ClubHouse Gothic Bold
ABCDEFGHIJKLMNOPQRSTUVWXYZ
abcdefghijklmnopqrstuvwxyz
1234567890?!~""{}

ClubHouse Serif light
ABCDEFGHIJKLMNOPQRSTUVWXYZ
abcdefghijklmnopqrstuvwxyz
1234567890?!~""{}

ClubHouse Serif bold
ABCDEFGHIJKLMNOPQRSTUVWXYZ
abcdefghijklmnopqrstuvwxyz
1234567890?!~""{}

These are our secondary alphabets. Use these for any
supportive information. The primary bounce type
is used for headlines. It's like eating too many french pastries
if we use it too much. They're great and wonderful, but
too much can make you sick.

KIT 8 — SECONDARY ALPHABETS

ClubHouse bounce

ABCDEF
OPQRST
abcdefgh
opqrstuv
123456 78

KIT 6 — PRIMARY ALPHABET

KIT 10 — 3D-NESS / SHADOWS

A Clubhouse is made of many parts. Rather than living
in a flat 2d world, we live in a 3d world. Elements, shapes,
words and characters are layered one upon another.
The shadows define the 3d effect.

KIT 11 — 3D-NESS / SHADOWS

There a
we mak
We can
Photo C
ability t

"Manuals don't make successful systems; people do."

—Sean Adams, partner, AdamsMorioka, Inc.

worked for me. If the logo is simple, the context it inhabits can be as complex or minimal as it needs to be. It's like plaid on plaid. A good logo is like a classic Armani black suit, or your favorite khakis. You can combine it with almost anything, and it still holds up.

Mnemonic value is critical. A logo can be beautiful, clever, and well made, but if the audience forgets it, it fails. Logos that are illustrations or answer every question (i.e. complex) also tend to be forgettable. If the mark is working too hard, telling the audience everything a company does and believes, it can't succeed. That's not a logo, it's a miniseries. The insistence on perfection addresses another trait that failed logos share: bad form. In my eyes, badly drawn curves, less than stellar letterforms, and clumsy proportions will quickly destroy a good idea.

New Technologies
Since that first logo and visual system for the Pacific Design Center more than a decade ago, technology and media have radically changed the way a company communicates with its audience. This has affected our processes, and the end results as well. Fifteen years ago we focused on print applications. That would

never work now. Our design process begins, not with how the logo looks, but how it will move and behave. It's presumed that the logo will need to animate, so we design a mark and visual system that incorporates animation and motion inherently. At the same time, a default mark must be able to exist in a small black-and-white newspaper ad. With the introduction of other media such as mobile devices, a simplified version, or type only version, of a logo is needed. What happens when the client can't use a logo, like the channel listing on an on-screen guide? That's when the importance of a good name becomes apparent.

One of the most apparent issues of identities for us is the importance placed on the system. The most critical components are color, type, and images. Color is the strongest tie to being memorable and portraying the right perception. Think of Tiffany blue. The color palette in the visual system should serve to reinforce and complement the primary identity. The color palette is also a primary signifier of the message. It tells us if the product or company is serious or humorous, fresh or traditional, positive or negative. Typographically, we incorporate a family of fonts that complements the logo. Using the same font for the logo and headlines takes away from the equity of the logo and dilutes its unique characteristics. Once again, it's about tone. Bembo communicates a very different message than Helvetica.

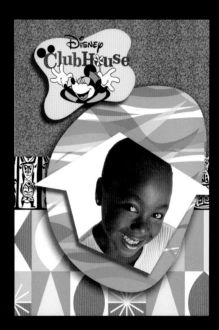

THIS SPREAD
The identity system for Disney ClubHouse consists of a static logo, and a changeable logo with a "magic knot-hole" incorporating characters. A color and pattern palette relies on colors and forms that clash. Most of the creative is handled by a variety of third party designers. The "clashing" elements allow for any combination to work. They are built to be dissimilar like a child's experience of piecing together a Clubhouse.

The style manual for Disney ClubHouse exists as a poster, and in booklet form. The instructions are presented with a tone that informs the overall system. Playful and spontaneous choices are suggested, using the visual system like a kit of parts to be assembled in any way.

PHILIP B.
SINCE 1991

Peppermint and
Avocado Shampoo

A Volumizing, Clarifying Shampoo

10% Pure Peppermint
& Plant Extracts
With Extracts of Peppermint and Avocado

8oz / 240ml
Made in the USA

PHILIP B.
SINCE 1991

Anti-Flake
Relief Shampoo

Heals and Soothes Dry Flaky Scalp

1% Pure Zinc Omadine
.525% Pure Coaltar
13.6% Pure Plant Extracts
with Extracts of Aloe Vera, Sage
and Juniper Berry

8oz / 240ml
Made in the USA

PHILIP B.
SINCE 1991

African Shea Butter
Shampoo

For All Hair Types
Normal to Color Treated

With Vitamin B5, 16 Plant Extracts
Fragrance Free

8oz / 240ml
Made in the USA

PHILIP B.
SINCE 1991

White Truffle
Moisturizing Shampoo

Safe for Colored
and Chemically Treated Hair

23.2% Pure Plant Extracts
With Extracts of Nettle and Thyme

8oz / 240ml
Made in the USA

PHILIP B.
SINCE 1991

Scent of Santa Fe
Shampoo

Gentle Daily Cleansing
For All Hair Types

10% Pure Plant Extracts
With Extracts of Piñon, Sage and
Juniper Berry

8oz / 240ml
Made in the USA

PHILIP B.
SINCE 1991

Chai Latte

Soul and Body Wash
A Deep Stimulating Cleanser

20%
Pure Botanical
Extracts

A Soulful Blend of Honey,
Milk Proteins, Black Tea,
Cardamon, Cinnamon,
Nutmeg, Ginger and
Black Pepper essential oils

12oz / 355ml
Made in the USA

PHILIP B.
SINCE 1991

Thai Tea

Body Wash™
A Cooling and Energizing Body,
Mood and Mind Cleanser

20%
Pure Botanical
Extracts

A Spiritual Blend of
Thai Tea, Honey, Coconut,
Milk Proteins, Peppermint,
Lemon Grass, Ginger Root
and Citronella extracts

12oz / 355ml
Made in the USA

PHILIP B.
SINCE 1991

Nordic Wood

One Step Hair & Body Shampoo
An Enchanting and
Grounding Journey

6%
Pure Nordic
Plant Extracts

A nurturing blend of
Norwegian Spruce,
Balsam Fir, White Pine,
Cedarwood and White
Camphor extracts

12oz / 355ml
Made in the USA

PHILIP B.
SINCE 1991

Chocolate Milk

Body Wash™
A Playful and Magical Experience

A Treat From
Your Nose to
Your Toes!

A nurturing blend of
Cocoa-Butter, Oat Protein,
Oat and Wheat Amino Acids
with moisturizing Aloe!

12oz / 355ml
Made in the USA

FOR EXTERNAL USE ONLY • DO NOT EAT • DO NOT DRINK

oh! Oxygen

very clear selecting the image attributes: style, black and white or color, candid or posed, wide shots or macro, the same photographer for all or a group of photographers. The content of the image choices can be politically touchy. Everyone can take a photograph, so everyone thinks he or she is an expert. It's also difficult to get beyond the content of an image, or the style. If someone hates a chair in an image, it can kill it. And finally, who is photographed? Do you have a good mix of men and women, racial divisions, age divisions? These are questions that must be weighed very heavily.

Launch

In addition to a standards manual, steps should be taken to maintain the consistency of the identity system. Whenever possible we manage the launch and initial use of an identity system. Some projects require that we release the system to an in-house department and other creative partners. This is where the science of systems applies. A well-designed system will inspire creativity and allow for flexibility while maintaining a strong proprietary perception. A system made too rigidly can lead to fast rebellion by the designers who take over the program. My philosophy for this hand off is pragmatic. In some instances, you simply need to let your children leave home and find their own way. Fast-moving media such as broadcast and online will begin to alter the system almost immediately. I was given a piece

of advice by broadcast pioneer Fred Seibert, "If it's right on television for fifteen minutes, you've done your best."

Controlling the logo and usage is challenging. For example, we designed a word mark for Aaron Betsky's book on gender and architecture, *Building Sex*. The cover and accompanying word mark worked well to enhance sales of the book, but the final product found its way into unexpected places. For example, the bright red cover and "Sex" word mark was used in a photo shoot for *Cosmopolitan* magazine. A scantily clad model is shown leaning suggestively against a bookcase holding the book as the primary prop. The article was "How to Pick Up Men in a Bookstore."

Young designers beginning to work in the field of identity should stop and ask questions. Build the criteria and thinking with the client before any visual studies begin. Nail down the attributes that the logo should address and make sure you have consensus with the client, and then start visual studies. Also, follow the three rules: simple, simple, and simple. How can you do more with less? All of the logic, and criteria, and systemic thinking involved in the making of an identity system are critical. But there is that one element, more important than any other: personal creativity.

OPPOSITE
A visual audit of packaging in the hair care industry showed that less expensive products had more flamboyant packaging. Philip B. is a high-end product selling at stores such as Barneys New York, Saks Fifth Avenue, and Bergdorf Goodman. The identity is a simple word mark with a classic and modern attitude. The other elements of the identity system, patterns, icons, shapes, and color combine to create a packaging line that remains direct without resorting to showy techniques.

TOP
Oxygen is a cable network that initially focused its programming toward a primarily female audience. Explorations for the logo included a simple ring shape that was set aside due to its lack of proprietary value. This exploration led to the sound of an "o." An exclamation mark was added to convey the network's energetic approach.

On screen graphics, print materials, and Web applications use the logo as the center of a response. The logo never is "slapped" onto a corner, but given life with a variety of audio cues ranging from surprise to amorous.

THIS PAGE
Via is a large line of paper products from Mohawk Fine Paper. The vastness of the line, seven finishes, twenty-eight tones, required a set of logos to identify each finish. They range in character to help with identification and clarity between finishes.

The relationship of the finishes to Via is expressed as a hub and spoke diagram on the website, rather than hierarchical. Each finish is given its own information page. The visual system also includes a set of mascots, including a squirrel and talking horse to explain the selection. The humorous and satirical copy is also a critical component of the Via identity system.

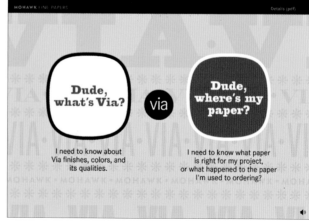

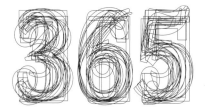

PENTAGRAM

Kit Hinrichs
San Francisco, California, U.S.A.

UNIVERSITY OF CALIFORNIA

uc**RIVERSIDE**

@issue:

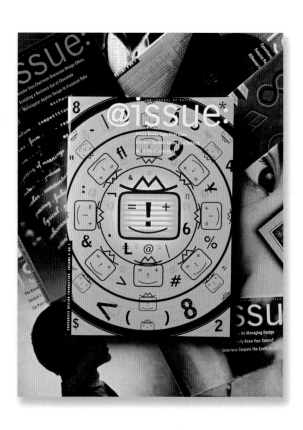

"A logo never stands alone. It is always part of a system."

—Kit Hinrichs, partner, Pentagram

Michael Johnson, London, United Kingdom

JohnsonBanks London, United Kingdom

Some designers believe that the hand of the designer should be invisible and no style should be imposed on a client. The other side of the coin is to use one unique style on all projects. Michael Johnson, cofounder of JohnsonBanks, designs logos and identity systems for clients that merge both philosophies. JohnsonBanks creates logos that are uniquely appropriate for the client, but the logos never fall into the banal or predictable.

OPPOSITE
Seven million people enjoy Pleasure Beach, an amusement park which has over 130 attractions. The park has a dozen roller coasters, including Europe's highest and fastest roller coaster, and cabaret, circus, and ice shows. The identity reflects Pleasure Beach's history but updates the forms for a younger attitude.

Johnson's logos are unexpected, yet they're also entirely appropriate. "Every time I think that I've fixed my view about how an identity should look, feel, or communicate, a new project will come along, and I'll realize that having no fixed modus operandi is what makes life so much more interesting."

Boring Words
Influential designer Bob Gill once said, "Boring words need interesting graphics." Johnson adheres to this when determining the choice of a symbol or word mark. But he just as quickly says, "The opposite also applies. My default setting is probably drawn toward word marks, but I know deep down that sometimes a symbol can be fantastically useful." He uses a symbol in situations where the name or messages of an organization don't communicate clearly. The logo for the Art Fund is an example of this solution. The symbol (about love and art) helped to differentiate the client in a crowded United Kingdom art funding and art charity market. A nondescript word mark might be lost in a competitive landscape.

Trying to narrow Johnson's philosophy into one simple approach is impossible. This is a key ingredient in his ability to create an identity that is unique and appropriate. While a symbol is used successfully to help communicate an oblique idea, a word mark is just as readily adopted in other situations. The logo for Shelter, a homeless charity,

draws power from its name. "Shelter is a great word that needs no extra identity baggage other than small typographic twists," Johnson explains. The same solution and reasoning are applied to the company More Th>n. The context of the logo and its applications provide another layer of meaning and message to this seemingly obvious logo. The success of this identity is based on its craft and Johnson's willingness to allow the words to do the heavy lifting.

Increasingly, varied technologies and media choices have led Johnson to rethink the idea of static logos. "I've been fascinated for years in identities that can change and adapt to their surroundings," Johnson says. "I'm thoroughly bored of the 'logo that goes in the corner' syndrome and I will do almost anything in my power to avoid this." The identity for BFI is an example. The simple application of a lens flare applied on the top of an image serves as a nontraditional logo. Johnson doesn't deny the ease of static logos. "Obviously one color, vector logos are fantastically easy to use and apply, but it doesn't always work out that way," he says.

Time and Place
Designers commonly attempt to do work that is timeless. Unfortunately, because we exist in a specific time and place, this can prove challenging. "Some might say I still naively cling to the idea that a good identity should stand the test of time, so it shouldn't

Addressing the issues
of homelessness and
unacceptable housing
conditions, Shelter is an
organization that helps
more than 170,000
people a year fight for
their rights and find
and keep a home. The
logo and identity system
have the same approach
as the organization;
it approaches the
challenge head-on
and without apology.

Most of the world knows
what a welcome mat
looks like. It's meaning
is clear. Switching the
word, "welcome,"
with the Shelter logo
communicates exactly
that; you are welcome.

"People just seemed to think I was nuts when I argued for logos that could change years ago."

—Michael Johnson, cofounder, JohnsonBanks

THIS SPREAD
The National Art Collections Fund had been the well kept secret of art funding in the United Kingdom for some time. With 80,000 members it provides an essential fund for U.K. galleries to keep works of art in the United Kingdom and on public display.

The logo communicates the idea of "loving" art plainly. There is no room for misinterpretation. The icon is mutable, allowing for multiple uses and variation.

Printed matter, such as posters and advertising combine the identity system with the objects it represents: painting, sculpture, and applied art objects.

ArtFunders this way

be too trendy or time-locked in its art direction style," Johnson says. "I love the idea that some of my work might last for decades, and sometimes it does." His approach to sidestep dated logos includes avoiding any digital effects that will stamp an identity with a kind of digital date. "I think the prevalence of three-dimensional logos now will look very early twenty-first century," he says. Johnson has also found a faster turnover for logos now, as opposed to longer-lived identities of the past. This, he claims, can be a positive. "Obviously a faster turnover is good for business and implies that identity design can be more of now and less classic," Johnson says. "But I still hold on to the idea that a good logo could last for ages."

The willingness to allow for change, the unexpected, and the accidental is inherent in Johnson's approach to an overall identity system. "As I've hinted, identities that are overly static and rigid strike me as inappropriate in the multimedia environment we now live in," Johnson says. "The schemes that are overly policed by in-house logo-cops are such a drag to work on for other design consultants. Before we became logo designers, we had to earn our spurs applying other people's schemes, and that was quite a salutary experience." The question posed, then, is how to maintain consistency and a clear message in a constantly changing environment, and with a variety of creative partners. Johnson's solution addresses the issue of the individual, rather than adding more rules to a rigid system. "The trick is

to make people want to get involved in a project, not just grin and bear it to pay the mortgage," he says.

Johnson's ability to design a logo to meet multiple challenges results in success. Failure occurs when a client demands mediocrity. Johnson's philosophy is direct. "I guess you could argue that organizations get the identities they deserve," he says. "It's probably no coincidence that dull, rigid, and formulaic organizations prefer dull, rigid, formulaic identities. There are some people that simply don't want to be interesting." The stellar reputation of JohnsonBanks attracts blue-chip clients with vision. Johnson's logos never repeat themselves, and they don't rely on a standard bag of tricks. The clients that work with Johnson hire him for his thinking, and they understand that the visual form is a product of this thinking. "Luckily, no one rings us up to tweak," Johnson says "No one sits in our studio and says 'Can you just repeat what you did for them for us?' They might admire the thinking that got us to a solution, but they never want the same solution."

Moving Ideas
The advent of motion graphics and the Web has meant Johnson is constantly thinking about how an idea will work in a moving or animated form. The logos are not designed in a static form and then animated. They are conceived as behaving

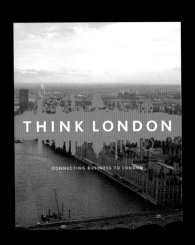

Think London is a campaign to sell the city as a premier location for global business. The campaign pitch, "Forget Paris, Berlin, and Beijing, set up in London instead," is distilled into one logo. Rather than using one symbol, such as Big Ben to represent London, there are forty-five.

The Strangest Place My Logo Appeared

Many, many years ago I worked in Sydney, Australia, and I designed a logo for one of Australia's biggest insurance companies, MMI. I was young, it wasn't that great (actually it was pretty awful), and I forgot about it. Twenty years later, I sat in a cinema watching some Hollywood blockbuster (I think it was *The Matrix*), and at the movie's finale that involved some very fancy special effects and a falling helicopter, I nearly fell out of my seat because there was my old, forgotten logo. The company had painted its logo on top of their building, and as Sydney had then become the city of choice to film blockbusters, there it was.

in motion from the onset of creative thinking. For example, the BFI logo began as an animation and was then repurposed as a logo. Johnson describes the shift in thinking, convergent with new technologies. "Changing technology has supplied the irrefutable reasons for flexibility that we've always desired," he says. "Before, flexible, changeable identity schemes were just limited to television broadcast companies. Now, everyone's interested in schemes that can adapt to their surroundings and appear less monolithic than before."

Because most logos and identity systems are eventually handed over to other creative partners, in-house departments, and advertising agencies, Johnson creates a unique kit of parts to maintain a cohesive message. "One of our most consistent approaches is unique, 'ownable' approach to typography," he explains. "If we can find a reason, or the money, we'll draw or modify a typeface." He also maintains a common and consistent set of criteria to create and select imagery. Color is a prevalent component of all Johnson-designed identity systems. "Sometimes color is paramount," Johnson says. "If a client inhabits a very color-coded sector, choosing a specific color to stand out is important."

The identity system's use on applications is a critical phase in Johnson's work. While

he doesn't find any specific applications to be more difficult than any other, the challenge becomes the maintenance after a logo is released. "The challenging part now is that virtually all of our systems are sooner or later handed over to in-house teams or the clients' day-to-day suppliers," Johnson says. "We're still learning how to get what's in our heads, and what seems natural to us, down on paper or on a PDF, in a way that can be followed, be inspirational, and not feel like a bunch of restrictions." The alternative is to use a few simple elements. But for Johnson, this is what leads to stale solutions. He finds the solution to be an inspirational identity system and staying involved with every project after its release. Johnson's approach is to do this, even if it is only a few hours a month.

The strategy of implementation is important to Johnson, but the designer inside describes his favorite logo application. "I'm a poster man, always will be," Johnson says. "When a client mentions 'posters,' my ears perk up immediately, and I've usually designed them by the end of the meeting."

Rules and Regulations
The systems manual is a document in transition. Some designers treat them as sacrosanct. Others believe they are now irrelevant. Johnson designs the standards manual, but he takes a more liberal app-roach than previous, immutable processes. He uses review meetings as a collaborative think tank to determine what is working currently, what has worked, and what

hasn't, and to decide what areas need more improvement, and whether to amend the guides. The JohnsonBanks office is built with metal walls. The designers regularly magnet up all the work in progress and collaborate with the clients. A negative is typically turned into a positive outcome with Johnson's attitude. "Some of our cultural clients often are short of money, and they can't afford to do the manual early," Johnson says. "That's meant we've had up to a year sometimes to try out the scheme and iron out any problems. It's quite an interesting way of working, actually."

As the design profession evolves, Johnson finds less interest in logo and identity design among students. "To be honest, in England at least, very few students seem to be interested in logos," he says. "This strikes me as a huge mistake. Their portfolios are crammed with ambient advertising, or viral online clips, or posters for film festivals, or personal projects. But they spend practically no time in art school thinking about identity, designing them, practicing them." The result of this lack of experience requires on-the-job training at JohnsonBanks. Johnson typically teaches young designers the process of logo making and identity from the ground up. "Brochures or websites all change," Johnson explains. "The one element that remains constant is the organizations' need to identify themselves in unique and interesting ways. In other words, identity design isn't going away. If our experience is anything to go by, it's getting more and more important."

Brando

1-31 July

Marlon Brando season
www.bfi.org.uk/brando
BFI Southbank
Belvedere Road
London SE1

Tickets 020 7928 3232

THIS SPREAD
The British Film Institute
is a well-known, but mis-
understood organization.
The Institute's activities
include publishing, the
London Film Festival,
Waterloo IMAX, and a
myriad of other activities.
The identity provides
visual glue holding
the many activities in
one place.

The logo is based on
the cinematic icon of
a lens flare. There are four
versions of the logo. They
all share the same lens
flare and letterforms, but
are oriented in different
directions to provide ease
of use to the designer
of any application.

A poster for a series of
films with Marlon Brando
exemplifies the change-
able lens flare logo and
typographic system. The
tone of all communica-
tions is minimal. The
Brando poster has two
primary messages: Brando
and BFI. There are no
other confusing elements
of communications added.

THEATRE

MODERN DOG

Robynne Raye and Michael Strassburger • Seattle, Washington, U.S.A.

Advice for Successful Logo Design

1. Find out the truth about the company or product and reflect that accurately in the identity. That will help to keep them focused.

2. This is more for the company or product itself, but it also applies to the identity: Look at the competition, find the hole, and fill that niche.

3. Of equal importance, the client must feel happy and comfortable with it, and it must work in the marketplace.

4. Get a true understanding of what the target market takes away on a first look at the identity.

5. Give weight to the client's ideas. They are more likely to be closer to their target market than you. Designers sometimes have an out-of-touch and elitist idea about their work. One of the biggest mistakes I see designers make is that they feel like "the client isn't sophisticated enough to get what I'm doing." If that's the case, then the target market probably falls into that same category. Hence the design isn't working.

6. At the risk of repeating ourselves we can't say enough how important it is to do your homework to get a full and accurate understanding of your client or product, their competition, and their niche in the marketplace.

green world now

Greenwood Park

™

Magic Board

C&G Partners New York, New York, U.S.A.

Steff Geissbuhler, Keith Helmetag, Jonathan Alger, and Emanuela Frigerio founded C&G Partners in 2005, after working together for decades at Chermayeff & Geismar. Their identity work is based on principles of clarity, simplicity, and universality. This approach has led to the creation of some of the world's most recognizable experiences.

OPPOSITE
The peacock was used by NBC in the early days of color television as a symbol of the transition from black and white to color programming, but not as a logo. After numerous unsuccessful attempts with logos using the company's initials, an abstracted *N*, and other imagery, the peacock was used as a pivotal icon for this large media network.

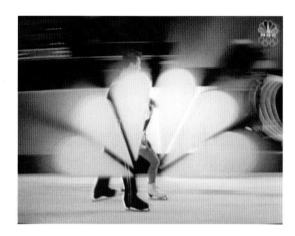

THIS PAGE
NBC recognizes that
each communication
contributes to the
overall impression of
the company. The new
identity is integrated
across all platforms,
including advertising,
marketing brochures,
stationery, business forms,
facilities and equipment,
and on-air animations.

The on-air animation
of the logo begins
with a variation of
the ubiquitous color
bars of television. they
quickly evolve into the
recognizable peacock
form, combining the
medium of television
to the NBC brand.

The identities clearly exemplify the concept
of a logo serving as a foundation for the
visual system. These marks are deceivingly
effortless. They share a commonality of
appearing to be the only logical option for
each client. C&G's experience and exceptional
skill create this illusion.

Nomenclature

Working with large-scale corporate
clients demands a high degree of clarity.
Nomenclature is often the first stumbling
block a designer can face. Often, the designer
speaks in one language, while the client
speaks in another. Geissbuhler begins
with basic definitions. "First, we establish
a nomenclature for what we generally now
call a logo or trademark," he says. "The word
logo is actually the Greek term for *word*, as
in Barneys New York, for example. We refer
to this as a word mark." Delineating the
nomenclature further, he adds, "A symbol
represents a recognizable thing, like a bird,
the sun, a forest, etc. The NBC peacock
is a good example. A mark on the other
hand is an abstraction, like the Chase logo,
which is meant to express a notion—in this
case enclosure, security, maybe even a coin."

There is no uniform answer to the word mark
versus symbol approach in Geissbuhler's
work. He believes a word mark is the simplest
and most direct way of identifying an entity;
no translation is necessary. The word mark
spells out the name and communicates the
client's business or qualities. In the instance
of a name being a common one, a word mark
will not suffice.

Geissbuhler's big picture thinking is apparent
in the instances where he has to create
a symbol. When the identity system includes
a variety of sub-brands or divisions, the symbol
is used to link all aspects to a parent company
or master-brand. "Very few symbols or marks
are identifiable and recognizable by themselves
without a name or word accompanying them,"
he cautions. "A mark, used by itself, needs
frequent exposure before it is associated
immediately with what it represents." The
NBC peacock is an example. This symbol is
given widespread and ongoing exposure on the
screen, in print, on signs, and in advertising.
Even in this global communication, the danger
exists that without the name NBC attached
to the symbol, some segments of the audience
may read television, but not NBC.

Geissbuhler designs a logo to be a visual
device, or shorthand for a company, organization, or product to identify, represent,
and communicate the brand. The logo is
a reduction of a complex message into a single
expression. It is the creation of a personality.
His pragmatic approach is as direct as the
focused logos he produces. Clients can think
of a logo as a magic bullet; one that will
solve every problem they have. Geissbuhler's
philosophy follows the theme that a logo
can never make a client's service or product
better than they were in the first place.
"A visual identity is like a sponge, absorbing
what we associate with a company's quality,
performance, and history," he explains.

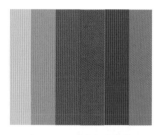

THIS SPREAD
The New York Public Library is a cultural attraction and a center for scholarship. To celebrate the library's 100th birthday, a special visual brand was designed to help launch an ambitious capital campaign. Rather than celebrate the past, the final graphic solution conveys the diversity of the institution's collections and holdings.

The logos forms, derived by treating each letter in the word "library" differently, suggests posters, rare books, braille, music, manuscripts, and digital files. The identity system is applied to a vast amount of collateral, including stationery, press kits, invitations, posters, banners, signage, and a line of branded merchandise.

Being Simple

One of the traits common to designers who excel at logo and identity work is an understanding of the need for simplicity in form. Geissbuhler's logo for Time Warner is a strong argument for this simplicity in design. The combination of an eye and an ear in restrained and uncomplicated form has proven to last longer and prove more flexible than more complex solutions. However, with today's technology in terms of reproduction techniques, different media, where graphics can move and morph, spin and blend, all variations are examined. Returning to the core message, Geissbuhler states, "It all comes down to what is appropriate to the project and makes sense. Simple logos are still the most memorable and iconic."

If an identity doesn't make a connection with something we can relate to, it fails. Richard Saul Wurman has said, "You understand something only relative to something you already understand." Geissbuhler's position on logos that fail relates to the idea that a good logo can never make a bad product good. The success or failure of a logo is inexorably linked to the product or service it represents. Other identities have failed because the service, product, or company it represented have failed. "I often use the example of Enron," he explains, "Paul Rand, one of the great graphic designers of the modern age, designed a beautiful logo for the Enron Corporation. Today that same logo stands for absolute corporate corruption."

Every identity Geissbuhler designs now needs to work on the Internet, in black and white or in a single color, low and high resolution, pixilated and be able to function in any other environment. "You should be able to embroider it," he jokes. Geissbuhler considers all of these applications and options in mind when initially designing the identity, rather than having to make adjustments later.

Building Blocks

Multiple elements such as typography, color, and imagery make a system that accompanies the logo. "The most challenging of these components depends on which one takes the lead and becomes the most important element next to the logo itself," Geissbuhler explains. If a color scheme or coding is part of the system, he finds the challenge to create a distinct, yet wide, palette that works in any combination and each media, and with each color being distinct from the other. "I do believe that the most challenging aspect to creating an identity system is to establish firm enough rules to guarantee consistency and at the same time to leave the door open for evolution," he continues.

Geissbuhler's identity systems would never succeed without clear guidelines that explain usage to other creative partners involved with a client. Typically, only the very basic standards are established in the beginning

THIS SPREAD
When Time Inc. and Warner Communications announced a merger, the new company lacked a trademark. Warner was primarily concerned with entertainment, Time with journalism. Their common denominator needed to be much broader: looking and listening, reading and hearing, receiving and sending.

The new logo is a pictograph combination of an eye and ear, the essence of communication. Originally associated with the corporate parent, the mark has now become the symbol for TimeWarner Cable, one of the most profitable divisions of the company.

The logo, a one color icon, is given power and variety with extreme scale changes and a commitment to high printing standards. This is critical, giving the logo the ability to maintain and strengthen proprietary value with a consistent and specific color of blue.

THIS PAGE
The Signature Theatre
Company name is
reversed out of a cloud
of signatures that extends
along the edges so
as to reveal the names
of several recognizable
playwrights. The typ-
ography stacks in such
a way that the first three
letters of the word *Theatre*
are set apart to allow for
the double reading of
The before the full name
of the company.

A vibrant palette is added
to the identity system,
further highlighting the
remarkable efforts of an
essential cultural venue
whose sustained artistic
excellence has generated
a deeply loyal following
among New York's highly
literate cultural audiences.

and are distributed in digital form, covering size restrictions, the relationships between the identity's various elements, secondary typography, and color. C&G also creates as many templates, prototypes, or actual applications as possible before publishing the graphic standards guidelines. This allows the identity system to be tested and able to evolve before firm rules are established. Both the basic standards and, later on, more elaborate guidelines with samples of applications are often published on a website. Another practice that has led to the success of Geissbuhler's identities is the advice given to clients that they revisit the identity elements and standards six months and a year after implementation.

While the process and reasoning behind each identity project is carefully constructed and maintains the highest degree of craft and logic, there is an obvious sense of joy inherent in Geissbuhler's work. This is most apparent in the resolution of the logo's applications. He describes which applications provide the greatest pleasure. "For a television network, I enjoy the animation of the logo," he says. "For a theater it might be the marquee or posters. For an art museum it might be the publication system. It really depends on what is the most visible and important application." This list repeats Geissbuhler's commitment to communication. Each identity has a specific message that is the priority, the media, or application that will be the predominant carrier of its message.

While Geissbuhler's identities are designed to function in multiple applications, there are unexpected instances that provide surprise. "We designed the identity for Mercy Corps a few years back and have since seen it applied to boats, latrines, food boxes, water pumps, bricks, and tents. Quite often it's painted by volunteers from memory on a wall, cloth, or a piece of wood. I've seen some pretty strange and entertaining interpretations of that logo," he recalls. And Geissbuhler's pet peeves? "I personally find doormats and elevator carpets a particularly strange place for a logo. Who wants to have their identities trampled and stepped on, all day long?"

The logos and identity systems designed by C&G Partners are among the world's most successful identities. The success of a logo, however, is directly connected to the product. "Just keep in mind that a trademark or logo don't always solve problems," Geissbuhler maintains. "It absorbs the quality and performance associated with its business, product, or service. Remember what happened to Paul Rand's beautiful Enron logo? Never mind the 3,000 year-old symbol of the swastika. We all know how that turned out."

Crane Paper is one of the United States' best known brand for high quality papers. The logo is a simplified icon of a bird, specifically a crane. The identity system includes the logo, typographic standards, colors, and production techniques. The promotions include a variety of techniques such as embossing and debossing to articulate the papers' quality.

The logo is applied as the primary image for the Crane Business Paper promotion. The tone of the materials is professional yet approachable. The choice to portray the brand as approachable with the open and simple logo, and pure colors is made to address a wider audience.

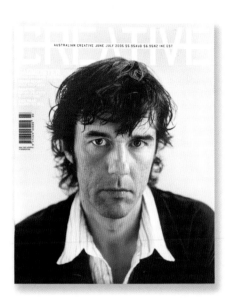

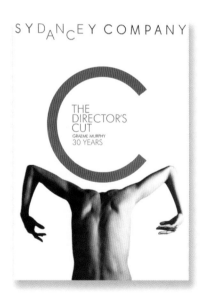

FROST DESIGN

Vince Frost

Surry Hills, New South Wales, Sydney, Australia

TOP
The identity for *Creative Magazine*, a publication that showcases a range of work as inspiration for creative professionals.

BOTTOM
Sydney Dance Company is Australia's premier contemporary dance company. The addition of the *A* and *C* on a lower baseline creates a combined read of the words *Sydney* and *Dance*, as well as an impression of movement.

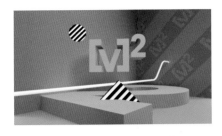

$\bigcirc\ \bigcirc\ \bigcirc\ \bigcirc\ \top$

COAST

Advice for Successful Logo Design

"It's about the methodical and analytical process of reduction. Simplification. It's also about working and learning from the people around you."

—Vince Frost, principal, Frost Design

FRANCO & CO

Boot

" " Swiss Re
, , Centre for Global Dialogue

INT
ER
NAT
FASHION
AL
GROUP

CHANNEL [V]™

Australian DESIGN AWARD ®

T IR III O

SYDNEY OPERA HOUSE

"Keep it simple. Make sure
it works in black and white.
Find the ultimate idea; an
identity is not just a logo."

—Vince Frost

freestyle

ty⌀o™

I MAGE
S OURCE

54

THE
LONDON
DESIGN
FESTIVAL
2003

LAURENCE KING
PUBLISHING LTD

MANTA

Imadesign Corp., Moscow, Russia

Erken Kagarov, founder of Imadesign Corp. in Moscow, approaches the design of logos and identities as if he were creating another reality. "The creation of visual style is like creating a virtual, imaginary world," he says. "I design this world's own language, rules, and culture." If this statement portrays Kagarov's process as fanciful or ungrounded, nothing could be less true. Kagarov insists that while this new reality requires a strong vision, hard work is a necessity for making this world real.

OPPOSITE
The Idea! festival, which is held in Novosibirsk, is the national advertising festival in Russia. The poster for the jubilee 10th festival introduces the logo in the midst of powerful and vibrant imagery.

This hard work includes determining the inhabitants of this world—who are the internal and external audiences? Who is the decision maker? Who are the stakeholders? Once these questions are answered, the task becomes finding the best way to communicate with each group. "Once I have made these determinations," Kagarov says, "then I find the exact image, or the distinct world, that can specifically express the idea of my client."

Following the concept of designing a language for a new reality, Kagarov believes it is important to remember the audience needs to be given a logo that "appears to have an interesting history. The logo's usage and applications should develop over time, appearing in different ways." He uses the analogy of a plot to describe the need for evolution and variety in usage of the logo. "Just like cinema, we need to maintain the interest of our audience," he says. "Consistency of language and visuals in a film is the same as consistency in a logo and identity system." This provides a continued interest in the logo and its applications, and it creates a style for all the elements in the service of the message.

Modernist Theory

Kagarov has no preset determination of a specific style for his logo design. "In our field, we are working to solve problems, that's why form should always be subordinated to the communication goals," he says. "Every logo must be designed into a form appropriate to the content. Simple forms typically are best, but due to the amount of logos in the world, this is sometimes challenging. Doing something simple and unpredictable is not easy." In basic terms, Kagarov is citing a primary modernist concept, "form follows function." Logos that fail are not designed to communicate, but for Kagarov, are designed with style that ignores the needs of the project. "Unsuccessful logos do not correspond to the client, company, or product," he explains. "For example, a logo may be complex and interesting with great flexibility, in an instance where only a simple reading is needed."

Digital media has changed Kagarov's approach to logo design over the past decade. He now believes a logo can be not only complex and polychromatic, but also changeable and dynamic. "Generally the whole world is changing," he says. "People are changing, and that has influence on both the logo and its implementation. This is about the characters and the plot of the story we are telling," Kagarov explains. Understanding the changing needs of culture and society, incorporating the shifts of audience usage and perception, and adapting the visual forms of a logo have been tools Kagarov has used to create some of Russia's best identities.

The Strangest Place My Logo Appeared
The strangest application of one of my logos was on the rug in front of the building entrance; everyone wiped their feet on the logo.
—**Erken Kagarov, founder, Imadesign Corp.**

национальный фестиваль рекламы идея!

THIS SPREAD
For advertising messages calligraphy was used to give special expression. Functional applications such as the website, use traditional typography from the identity system's elements.

A one color version of the image functions as a logo on merchandise. The simplified forms retain their message and create a strong solution.

Applications use traditional Russian motifs and focus on the primary image, a combination of a nested doll and light bulb. This expresses the process of creativity, and the need to go deeper into ones head to find ideas.

The star, which is the main element of the logo, is painted to give the sense of spontaneity and energy. Bright and multi-colored, the logo creates a fresh and dynamic image of the Idea Festival.

 атласлюкс

"I enjoy doing what I haven't done before."

—Erken Kagarov, founder, Imadesign Corp.

THIS SPREAD
Atlus Lux Kitchen Furniture Stores is a leader in the market of Russian kitchen furniture manufacturers. The symbol represents a combination of two Russian capital letters from the name and is reminiscent of the light rays of a kitchen lamp. The word mark is built with the Univers typeface which has a highly refined family of different weights.

A style guide maintains consistency with the logo and its applications. Photographs of vegetables are selected to correspond to the identity systems' colors. The vegetables are associated with growth, cooking, and the kitchen They are successful brand identifiers, increasing recognition in tandem with the logo.

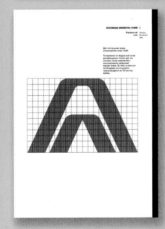

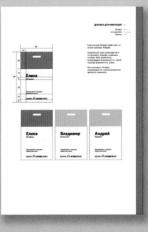

Storytelling

Kagarov uses the elements of a system as parts of the storytelling experience. The new world, or reality, that he is creating is populated with the audience and the end users. The logo is the center of this world, and the elements are the settings, props, and costumes. "Color is the most active sign for the audience," Kagarov says. "It creates instant recognition and provides a sense of possibility." Typography and image selection are also important elements used to create a fully realized identity system. Once the design components are assembled, Kagarov determines how pieces in the identity will be printed, aiding in the tactile experience of the identity, which can range from silkscreen, offset lithography, and letterpress to digital reproduction.

"The most difficult aspect of designing an identity system is to determine how all the components can create effective communica- tion as a whole," Kagarov explains. The overall and holistic communication is created by the appropriate usage of all elements, skillfully combined. "A visual system should be integral and harmonious, but at the same time dynamic and changeable," he describes.

Kagarov's solutions typically appear to have a light touch. They are never desperate, overworked, or self-important. "I think one of the most difficult things in logo design," he says, "is to find the solution that, on one hand creates a precise communication for the product or service, and on the other hand, is vivid and innovative." The successful solution for Kagarov is not only in the hands of the designer. His experience has led him to understand that the logo and the company or product it represents are intrinsically connected. If a client has a message or product that is not unique, it is impossible to create a logo and identity that will convey something different and original. The lack of definition causes, for Kagarov, "a situation that produces identities for similar companies that look like twins." His solution is to work on interesting projects with non-typical clients. This will, almost always, create an unexpected solution for the designer and the client.

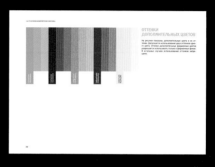

позитроника

THIS SPREAD
The store design for Positronika uses the primary identity colors, light green, white, and black to identify zones. Supplementary colors are used for identification of sales area zones to simplify navigation. Each product group uses a unique color and pictogram. This reinforces the digital and technical focus of the brand.

The systems manual is a guide to the logo usage, identity elements, and color code requirements. It is presented in a simple and clean fashion, reflecting the simply and "friendly" tone of the logo.

Reflecting the wide range of goods, simplicity of choice, and pleasure of purchasing, the symbol is dynamic, bright, and multicolored. It is a string of interlocking lines that has a *festival* nature. The symbol is related to the structure of the atom, which reflects the store's technical orientation.

The interiors use identity elements and maintain the theme of openness and friendliness.

Medved Vodka is a "lux" class vodka brand for the Republic of Kazakhstan market. The logo and identity elements are associated with vodka of Russian origin and create a strong and vivid image. The iconic bottle shape underlines product purity and transparency. One year after being introduced Medved Vodka became the leading vodka brand in the Republic of Kazakhstan.

THIS PAGE
RBT provides a full range of services to business with trip planning and management of corporate travel expenses. The logo's dotted line represents RBT's three main services: reservations of air tickets and hotels, visa management, and organization of conferences.

The World Financial Center

DOYLE PARTNERS

Stephen Doyle
New York, New York, U.S.A.

THIS PAGE
The World Financial
Center is a complex
of buildings in Lower
Manhattan. The complex
is home to several major
corporations, fine dining
experiences, arts events,
and shopping. The logo
illustrates the various
aspects coming together
as a unified idea.

OPPOSITE
The U.S. Green Building
Council (USGBC) is
a nonprofit organization
committed to expanding
sustainable building
practices. The logo
represents the mission
to advance structures
that are environmentally
responsible, profitable,
and healthy places to
live and work.

U.S. GREEN BUILDING COUNCIL

USGBC

SM

Top Five Rules for Logo Design

1. A logo should tell a story, whether it is pictorial or not.

2. It should not tell the *whole* story, it cannot. If it did, it would be a book, not a logo.

BARNES&NOBLE
BOOKSELLERS

"God is in the retail."

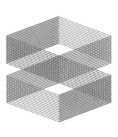

TISHMAN SPEYER

Nº 01

DWR **PROFILE**

THE PROFESSIONAL RESOURCE FROM DESIGN WITHIN REACH
U.S. $7.50

DESIGN WITHIN REACH

DWR Profile:
A New Resource for
Design Professionals

DWR was conceived from the outset four years ago as something "by designers
for designers." Many helped us shape our business: Kit Hinrichs at Pentagram
for our graphic identity, and numerous product designers, architects, and interior
designers have made us what we are today. And design-oriented businesses
are the foundation of our customer base; we have over 30,000 business clients,
ranging from prestigious universities and nationally known retailers to local
health clubs and restaurants. (See pages 8-9).

To show our appreciation, we are launching a new service this year specifically
for Design Professionals: Profile. The service includes this publication (designed
by Morla Design), and an annual catalog Workbook (designed by Pentagram and
[...] publications are focused on our community, with profiles of designers and
[...] events and places of interest, case studies on some aspect of the world
[...] sharing their thoughts on some aspect of the world
[...] available in April) organizes our products by
[...] clients to find what you need (see
[...] each one is contract qual[...]
[...] ness client[...]

Jennifer Morla, San Francisco, California, U.S.

Morla Design, San Francisco, California, U.S.A.

A Chinese proverb says "the reed that does not bend will break." Jennifer Morla applies this thinking to her logos and specifically, identity system design. When Morla Design was founded in 1984, this philosophy was in contradiction to all accepted identity rule. Logos and identity systems were historically rigid and unchangeable. A system in 1960 might be as simple as a black-and-white logo, and a system of Helvetica and navy blue only. With the introduction of additional media and greater technological choices, this attitude began to change.

OPPOSITE
Recognizing the need to strengthen their appeal to the design professional, DWR Profile addresses topical design and architecture issues and showcase mid-century classic and contemporary furniture and products.

The applications, including this sixteen page semi-annual magazine, contains relevant case studies and interviews, and highlights products and company benefits.

The need for flexibility was also demanded by a rise in the "creative" class. As nondesign professions, such as medicine, finance, manufacturing, and law were encouraged to explore creative thinking, the concept that each individual in society was creative has expanded. Morla's response was to embrace a company's message, but to allow the identity to be flexible. "A good logo should reveal the character of the company or brand," she explains. "It should reflect their DNA, but it should be flexible and adapt to a variety of applications. I try to create a visual vocabulary that is adaptable in a variety of media."

Symbols

Morla's design process is rooted in an analytical and methodical philosophy. The seemingly simple determination of a symbol or word mark is as carefully considered as the critical messaging. "Both symbols and word marks can be equally successful. Each have limitations," she explains. "A symbol often can be scaled down to a quarter inch, making it very appropriate for digital and online applications. The downside to a symbol is that it has to be supported by consistent, large scale, and mass marketing for the public to recognize and identify the company or brand."

The concept of fluidity is infused into all of Morla's logos. Many of her logos are allowed to be one color, two color, multicolored, animated, morphed, spun, and make sound. She describes the need for fluid systems with the same passion she has for color and vitality in the logos. "I think rigid confines were more appropriate prior to the advent of the digital era," she says. "For a logo to succeed in both print and Web environments, it must be able to evolve. It should succeed in one color or full color, and it should be able to move and animate in a way that reveals and surprises." The willingness to allow this radical flexibility is not a freeform, anything goes response. Morla creates accompanying visual systems that support the logo, providing a strong foundation. "The burden of creating a successful corporate or brand identity should not fall on the logo itself, but in the successful implementation of a design language and visual system that supports the logo," she explains. The understanding of inherent limitations of the logo as a singular object is one of the qualifying elements of Morla's expertise in logo and identity design.

Fluid Systems

Echoing Morla's philosophy that rejects a rigid and didactic approach, her attitude toward the visual system looks in the opposite direction from the immutable systems of the 1950s and '60s. Once again, a system of Helvetica, navy blue, and a twenty-four-pica rule at the edge of every page will not function with the multiplatform needs today. Morla creates not a visual system, but a visual language. Her visual systems encompass a vocabulary of fonts, colors, patterns, photographic or illustrative styles that complement each other, communicate the business, and enhance the logo. These elements are then applied in a unique and thoughtful way to promote the message of the brand.

Morla cites numerous instances where a well-conceived logo was applied over and over again as the sole design element on a plethora of corporate and consumer applications. The applications must maintain the same level of care, as the logo itself. Morla uses the example of carpeting. "Is it really appropriate to slap a logo on a carpet and have the audience walk all over it?" she asks.

Increasingly diverse technologies have expanded the opportunity for communication. Morla anticipates the broad range of applications as a logo is being conceived. While other designers may design a logo and then create versions for different media, Morla integrates the need for multiple versions into the earliest explorations. "The applications for each logo now are broad: animation, signage, packaging, even creating the building barricade graphics," she says. "All of these have unique confines that allow for a new expression of the identity."

Morla's identity system for Wells Fargo Bank reached every consumer touch point for Wells Fargo Bank. She designed and oversaw production on all credit cards, ATM cards, ATM signage, brochure systems, proprietary check designs, branch signage, wayfinding systems, and private banking materials, all of which created a unified system for "the oldest bank in the West." This serves as a pivotal example of Morla's ability to maintain the integrity of a logo, while allowing flexibility in the system. The Wells Fargo Bank materials remain fresh and creative, without falling into the predictable and dull. They do this and create equity for the brand and the logo.

THIS PAGE
Infuselle is an upscale
product line from Shaklee,
a mail order beauty and
health care company.
The logo's forms are
repeated in the design
of the packaging, and
the shapes of the bottles:
rectangles and circles.

The Infuselle identity
system includes color,
typography, shapes,
and materials. The bottle
caps are color coded
with specific anodized
metal tones to identify
skin type categories.

I call my jeans "real slow now"

I named my creation "sweetne...

I dubbed my jeans "soul patch"

I named my jeans "apartment hu...

Levi's® Original Spin™
create your own jeans

THIS SPREAD
The logo and identity system for Levi's Original Spin reflect the nature of the product, custom designed jeans. The concept of the consumer as creator of their jeans is enhanced by the word mark and imagery. The black-and-white photographs, a key component of the system, represent the many types of personalities and individual and style options of the product.

Wells Fargo Bank

THIS PAGE
From its founding in 1852, during the California Gold Rush, Wells Fargo earned a reputation of trust by dealing rapidly and responsibly with people's money and goods. This history, and the ethos of the American West inform the design of the Wells Fargo identity and collateral materials. The script word mark is derived from forms originally drawn in the 19th century. It reflects the company's values and history. The imagery and color palette of the system further reinforce the bank's philosophy and heritage.

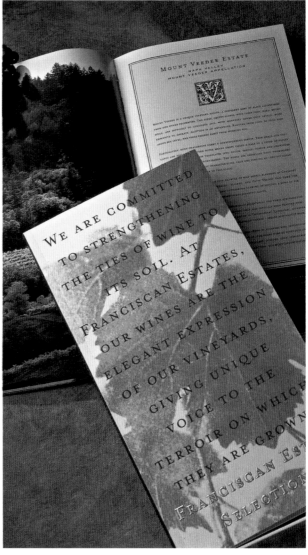

Morla Designisms

1. Design does not live in an aesthetic vacuum. Design is influenced by and influences contemporary society.

2. Design is not solely a marketing device that supports consumerism. It can be a communicator of dissent; it can market ideology. It can affect change.

3. Design must surprise and inform.

4. Design can be seductive propaganda. It is our responsibility to be knowledgeable about what we are asked to communicate. Make your decisions educated decisions.

5. Design has a rather symbiotic relationship with style, and style is somewhat precarious. What looks great today may look silly in fifteen years, and maybe if you're extremely lucky and talented, it will look good again in twenty. Great design is, quite simply, innovation that reflects the spirit of an era and becomes a classic because of its timeless appeal.

6. Question the need for any piece of print communication. This is the most elementary way of protecting the environment. Often, the communication can be executed in a much more meaningful way that goes beyond traditional design vehicles.

7. Respect the power of printing. A piece of paper doesn't necessarily go away. That message, that image, with your name proudly credited in four-point type, may last decades. It's a humbling thought.

8. Multiplicity works. Sol LeWitt knew it when he lined up 100 white boxes on a floor. Bruce Mau knew it when he put hundreds of big, grainy pictures back to back for Rem Koolhaas, and the Gap knows it when they fill their windows with hundreds of kids' sneakers.

9. Find your own voice by experimenting, by allowing the time to experiment, and by taking risks. This is why being in school is a luxury. School allows you the structured time to research, analyze, synthesize, ideate, strategize, and create. This is what being a designer is all about.

10. Design that moves others comes from issues that move you.

11. No design is completely original. We are all influenced by the bombardment of visual information we are exposed to on a daily basis. But understand that influence and plagiarism are two different things.

12. A good designer is a great listener. And if you listen smartly, the client nearly always tells you the solution.

13. A good designer is a great storyteller. Every company, service, and institution has a story to tell. Explore the narrative and banish the banal corporate speak we've read a million times before.

14. Accidents often produce the best solutions. And accidents are a hands-on experience. Only you can recognize the difference between an accident and your original intent.

15. Collaboration is good.

16. Passion enables us to remain true to our creative vision. Analyze, synthesize, visualize, but don't compromise.

17. Extremes work: really large, or really thick, or really small, or really colorful, or really simple, or really dense.

18. We are the creators of artifacts.

19. Designing takes time.

20. Ideas come faster the older you get.

21. Asking questions generates more ideas.

22. "Seriously funny" works.

23. Dichotomy works. Try juxtaposing opposites: the historical with the vernacular, the rough with the refined, the brash with the sublime.

24. The space in between is as important as the space occupied.

SEABLUE MGM GRAND HOTEL, 3799 LAS VEGAS BLVD, SOUTH
LAS VEGAS, NV 99109 702 891 7711 WWW.MGMGRAND.COM

SEABLUE
MGM GRAND HOTEL
3799 LAS VEGAS BLVD, SOUTH
LAS VEGAS, NV 89109

SEABLUE

JAY WETZEL, EXECUTIVE CHEF

MGM GRAND HOTEL 3799 LAS VEGAS BLVD, SOUTH
LAS VEGAS, NV 89109 702 891-7711 WWW.MGMGRAND.COM

Sea Blue is a fish restaurant at the MGM Grand in Las Vegas, Nevada. A signature visual element in the restaurant is a 120-foot (3.7m) sardine tank. The logo and identity system "ride the horse the direction it's going." The system does not layer a new visual element onto the restaurant. Morla uses the most recognizable and memorable part of the experience, the sardine tank, and lets that form the foundation of the identity. The color palette follows the same logic, and based on a variety of blue tones.

My First Logo

My first job after receiving my design degree was as a designer for PBS in San Francisco. I had to create logos for each program produced. That included applications to all traditional print: press kit covers, stationery, posters, and advertising. But the true excitement was animating the logo for the show's opening sequence. This was back in the seventies, when television and film were the only mediums that required animation. Creating the animation of type was all done by hand cutting individual letters of photo-type and photo stat artwork, each captured as still video frames. And this animation of type and imagery had to be communicated by producing frame-by-frame storyboards to engineers, who would, fingers crossed, do the design justice.

SEABLUE

OPTION 1

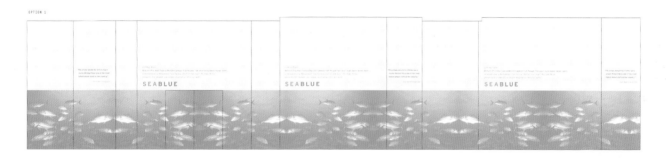

OPTION 2

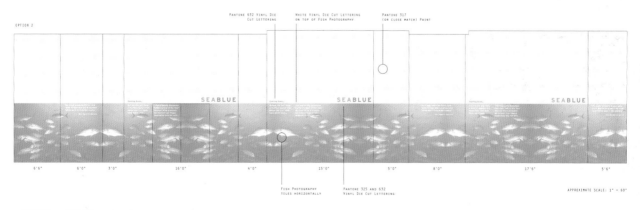

PANTONE 632   PANTONE 325   PANTONE 317

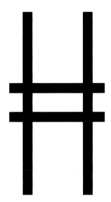

PENTAGRAM

Paula Scher
New York, New York, U.S.A.

The Most Important Things to Know before Beginning to Design a Logo

1. What is the spirit of the organization or corporation?
2. Who is the audience?
3. Who are their competitors?
4. What is the visual language of that milieu?
5. Who is making the decision about which logo is picked?
6. How will the logo be most often used? What other components
   are needed to make it understandable as a system?

curiouspictures

The **Met**
ropolitan
Opera

TIFFANY & CO.

PENTAGRAM

Michael Bierut
New York, New York, U.S.

Top Ten Logo Design Rules

1. A logo isn't everything. A company's image is the sum total of many different factors. Sticking a clever logo on a stupid piece of communication gets a client nowhere. Make sure that the company looks, sounds, and feels smart in every way, every time it goes out in public. This is actually better than a logo.

2. Relentless consistency is your secret weapon. Companies with strong graphic identities have built them through years of use. Here's some free advice. Pick a typeface. Pick a color. Use them over and over and over again, on everything. Before long you'll find yourself with an identifiable look and feel. Again, this is more valuable than a logo,

3. Don't assume that shapes and colors have magical meanings. Does baby blue say "luxury" to you? It does when it's on a box from Tiffany. The Nike executives who picked the swoosh did it as a reluctant compromise; what they really wanted was stripes, like Adidas. Logos are just holders for meaning. It's the company that gives meaning to the logo, not the other way around.

4. Be simple. Some of the best logos are the simplest logos. One of the oldest is the mark used by the Bass brewery: It's a red triangle. Target has made a red circle with a red dot in the middle seem the very essence of affordable, hip practicality. Now H&R Block is trying to claim a green square. It will probably work. Simple things are and easy to remember and tend not to date as quickly

ABOVE
Based on the original identity design, the Saks Fifth Avenue mark was refined and presented with a contemporary feel by use of strong contrasted letterforms that, when segmented and rearranged, became more about the identifiable shapes and compositions.

5. Leave it open. Don't try to make a logo that will explain at a glance to everyone who sees it the complete nature of your company's history, its business plan, its organizational structure, and its product lines. You will not succeed. This is a good thing. A logo that raises a question and is open to interpretation is better than one that attempts to contain all the answers.

6. Know your audience. Who is your audience? The whole wide world? Or just a few dozen customers? Too often, logo design is an internal exercise with predictably arcane results. Never forget that at the end of the day, the design that you do only works when it works for people who haven't been in all the meetings, and who are just going to encounter your message briefly in the course of a busy day.

7. Do good work.

8. Don't be embarrassed. Well-made and attractive is better than cheap and ugly. This is true for products, and it's true for the tools you use to communicate. Quality counts. Everyone's got a budget. Consider doing a little bit less and a little bit better. Make everything used to communicate as good as it can be. Logos and colors can be considered cosmetic, and hardheaded business people sometimes avoid focusing on them. But most design-driven companies got that way thanks to a highly-placed advocate, from Thomas Watson at IBM in the sixties, to Steve Jobs at Apple today. For a design program to work, it needs to be seen as important to important people. Care about it.

9. Get good advice. Common sense works well. But sooner or later, a professional graphic designer is needed for help. AIGA is the largest professional organization for graphic designers. The AIGA website, www.aiga.org, has advice about how to find and work with them.

10. Be a good company. IBM President (1952–1971), Thomas Watson Jr. is credited with saying, "Good design is good business." He also pointed out that a good design can help a bad product fail faster. Your brand is a promise. It's up to you to see to it that your products and services deliver on that promise. America's all-time greatest logo designer, the late Paul Rand, created logos for IBM, Westinghouse, ABC Television, and UPS. His last logo was for a company you may have heard of called Enron. It's actually a good logo.

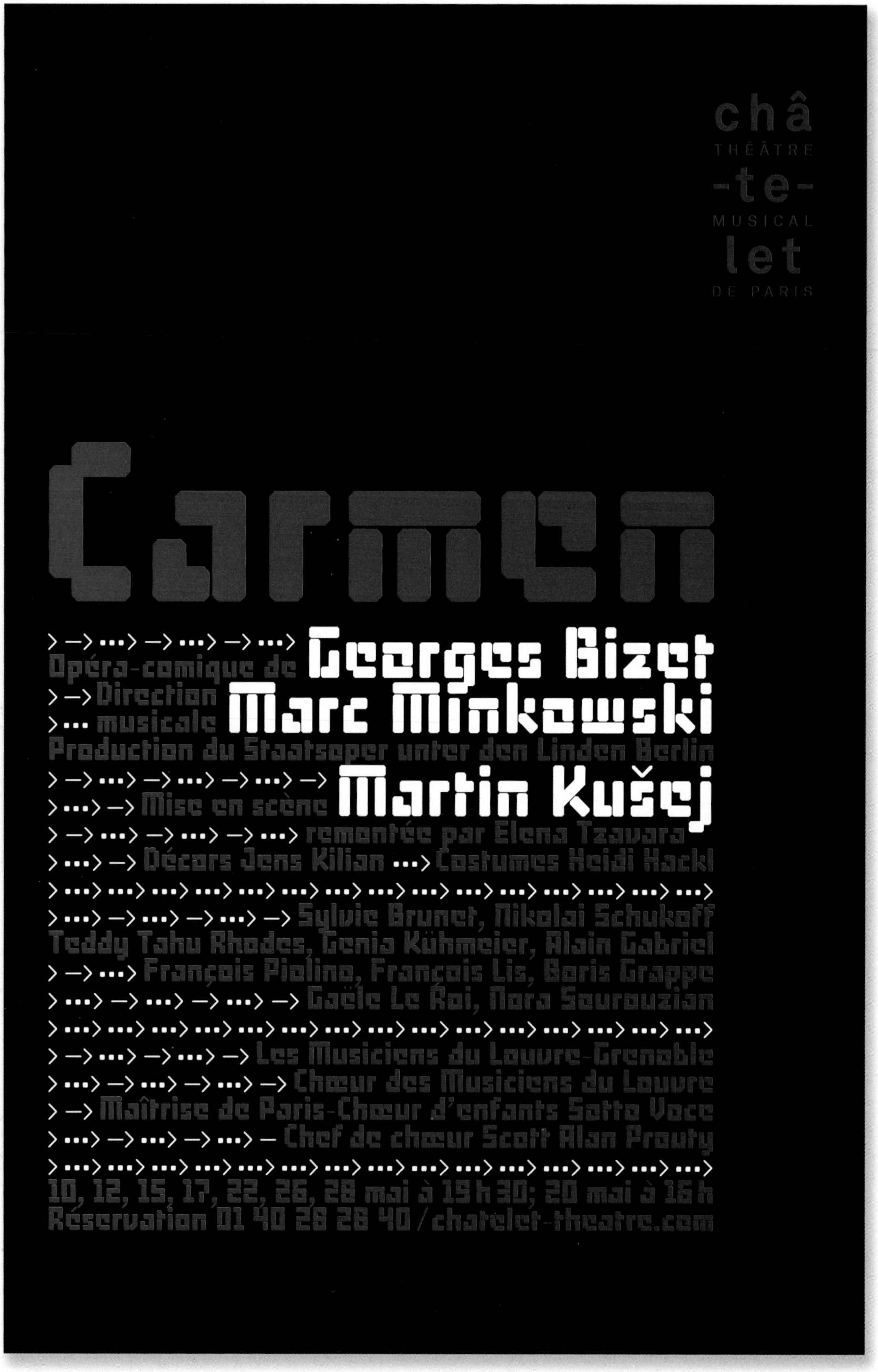
châ
THÉÂTRE
-te-
MUSICAL
let
DE PARIS
Carmen
Georges Bizet
Opéra-comique de
Direction
musicale
Marc Minkowski
Production du Staatsoper unter den Linden Berlin
Martin Kušej
Mise en scène
remontée par Elena Tzavara
Décors Jens Kilian
Costumes Heidi Hackl
Sylvie Brunet, Nikolai Schukoff
Teddy Tahu Rhodes, Genia Kühmeier, Alain Gabriel
François Piolino, François Lis, Boris Grappe
Gaële Le Roi, Nora Sourouzian
Les Musiciens du Louvre-Grenoble
Chœur des Musiciens du Louvre
Maîtrise de Paris-Chœur d'enfants Sotto Voce
Chef de chœur Scott Alan Prouty
10, 12, 15, 17, 22, 26, 28 mai à 19 h 30; 20 mai à 16 h
Réservation 01 40 28 28 40 / chatelet-theatre.com

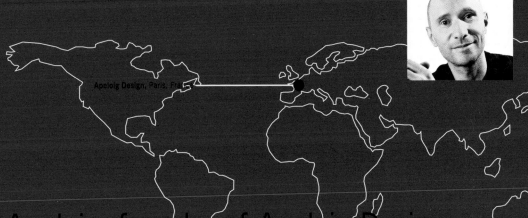

Apeloig Design, Paris, France

Philippe Apeloig, founder of Apeloig Design, has an approach to logo design that is, like his aesthetic, clear, and undeviating. He stresses issues such as clarity, curiosity, and being recognizable. His logos are unapologetic, speaking to the audience without explanation, but with a powerful impression. From an analytic perspective, an Apeloig-designed logo commits to reaching a design that is conceptual, sober, and witty. It is designed to live a long time, and for that reason it never comes from trends.

OPPOSITE
A performance poster for Chatelet, a musical theater of Paris, utilizes a defined system of defined graphic layouts, a unique typeface, and limited color palette.

> "Designing any logo, whether a symbol or a word mark, has to do with the awareness of written language as visual communication. You have to be direct, more and more clearly. You must never be traditional—always avant-garde!"
>
> —Philippe Apeloig, founder, Apeloig Design

It is never ordinary, but it will soon become familiar. And it is the foundation to a system that supports multiple applications. "The structural frame of every identity system must be invisible," Apeloig says.

Overuse and Abuse

A logo should create an immediate dialogue between the designer, the company, and consumers. For Apeloig, at times, a symbol reveals a meaning better than a word or a series of words. It could be used as a pictogram or an ideogram, similar to hieroglyphics. "The essence of a symbol is the form, the shape, the proportions, the abstract idea," Apeloig says. "Of course, some symbols have been used so much that they become boring or lacking in novelty. We think that we know them already. Only if the style or the graphic aspect is innovative can it become a new visual identity." This is the crucial question for every designer: How do I make something appear fresh or have a new layer of meaning when it has been used so many times? Apeloig compares the challenge with the difficult exercise of designing a chair. A chair is a simple piece of furniture. How can a designer make it appear new, with a unique form?

The same challenge exists for word marks. While letters are already symbols that anyone who knows how to read can decode, Apeloig believes that the design must be deliberate and innovative to make a word mark extraordinary. "A successful word mark must be overdramatic, intricate, or have spectacular effects if it is to appear as remarkable as a purely symbolic mark," he says. "The strong use of typography is critical. It must result in a dynamic composition, regardless of the typeface or the style of type that is used."

Apeloig uses simplicity and reductive aesthetics in much of his work. His logo designs are no different. He believes a logo does not seek to command the viewer's attention, just to hold it. While the logo's use and its combinations can be complex, diverse, and rich, a successful logo is like the foundation of a building. "The more stable this foundation is, the higher you can go," Apeloig says. Logos that fail are unmemorable or too difficult to understand. These can be badly drawn, too complex, or have clumsy proportions creating a situation that will not allow for innovation. The logo is failed before it is launched.

The Space/Time Continuum

New technologies and media have not changed Apeloig's design of identities. "I look for an inexhaustibility of the modern language of design and feel comfortable in its alliance with the classical rules of formal language," he says. "I try to create links with the modernist past without ignoring the fact that technology has dramatically changed our vision for design and the way we communicate." Amidst the proliferation of media, Apeloig enjoys the new artistic process and infinite possibilities in the creation of animation. He uses this as

THIS SPREAD
The Châtelet system included a strict color palette with a mixture of alarming, eye catching colors and complementary calming earth tones.

Printed collateral, such as this brochure, used limited resources without sacrificing the distinct look for the theater.

An unexpected execution for the seasons brochure added to the unique and proprietary qualities of the identity system.

a medium to find a new space for experimentation, using art and aesthetic motion in sensory psychology. This medium has transformed many of Apeloig's identity systems into kinetic works based on the concepts of space, motion, color, and light.

The critical component of an Apeloig visual system is the capacity for the logo to mutate and evolve over time without losing its clarity. A logo cannot escape its functionality as a necessary design element. It needs to ignore trends and explore the infinite combinations of its possible evolutions, while maintaining its identity over time. One of the solutions to aid in this ability is a complete and consistent design system. "Every visual element must connect, whether that means repeating the same identical element or creating patterns, symbols, or systems that work well together," Apeloig explains. "The logo must be the key to the entire system, summing up everything you mean to say about the company at once." Regardless of the element or application, all of Apeloig's pieces work together to maintain a cohesive message.

Ouverture
15 septembre
1998

Musée
d'art et d'histoire
du Judaïsme

3O3

THIS PAGE
A quarterly magazine dedicated to fine arts of Pays de la Loire area, the 303 magazine identity is based on the sum of the area's departmental codes. This is shown conceptually by simply modifying the '0' as parts coming together.

With the identity occupying a limited amount of vertical space, the cover designs of the magazines are able to have unique design from issue to issue.

The creation of a consistent and united message is one of Apeloig's most difficult but exciting challenges. With a good logo, it is easy to be inspired with new ideas for applications and uses. This can be fun and interesting, but in the end, the message may not be connecting and the viewer may not feel the full impact of the visual system. "With a great logo, the system should come together almost naturally," Apeloig says. "The original idea is so good that the rest of the system feeds into it naturally."

Maintenance

Apeloig's standards manuals are distilled to the minimum guidelines necessary to ensure that the identity system will never be mishandled. In the act of working with the logo, the end user must not be drawn into a complex and heavy system. If the logo is stable and clear, it is easier for the end user to maintain the consistency of the identity system. However, a visual identity carries a fragile dimension that needs to be checked and supervised regularly. Apeloig advises each client to have an art director pay attention and protect the integrity of the visual identity while seeing that it is not frozen and static, but lively and fresh.

octobre en normandie. 1er - 31 octobre 1992

13, rue Poret de
Blosseville
76100 Rouen.

locations:
Rouen: 35 70 04 07
Le Havre: 35 21 41 21
Dieppe: 35 82 04 43

musique et danse

octobre

Jean-François Chougnet
Commissaire général

AFAA
Association française d'action artistique
1bis avenue de Villars
75007 Paris

T +33 (0)1 40 03 74 72
F +33 (0)1 53 69 83 93
jf.chougnet@villette.com

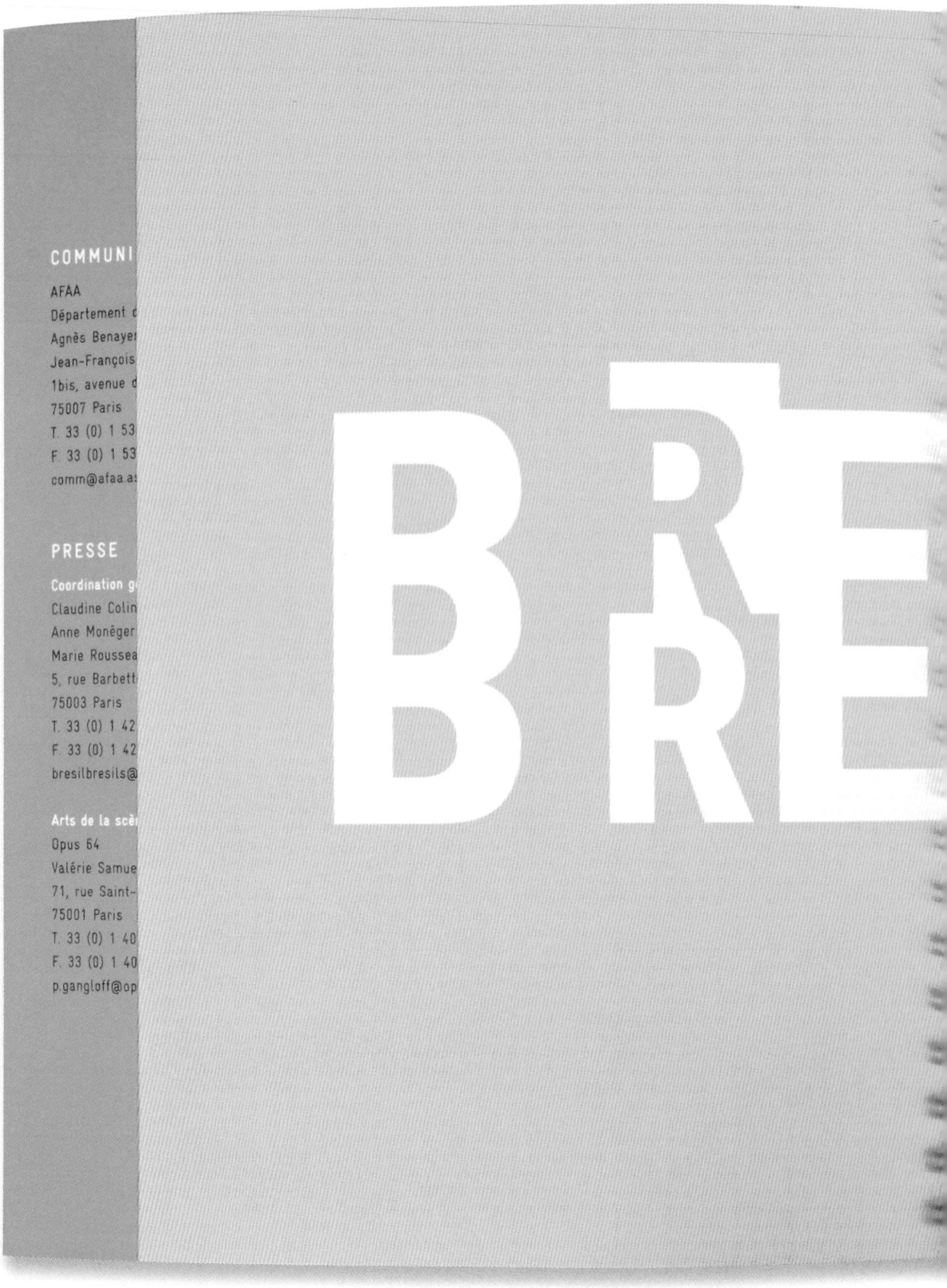

Année du Brésil en France

COMMUNI

AFAA
Département d
Agnès Benayer
Jean-François
1bis, avenue d
75007 Paris
T. 33 (0) 1 53
F. 33 (0) 1 53
comm@afaa.as

PRESSE

Coordination g
Claudine Colin
Anne Monéger
Marie Roussea
5, rue Barbett
75003 Paris
T. 33 (0) 1 42
F. 33 (0) 1 42
bresilbresils@

Arts de la scè
Opus 64
Valérie Samue
71, rue Saint–
75001 Paris
T. 33 (0) 1 40
F. 33 (0) 1 40
p.gangloff@op

Inspired by Brazilian visual
and aural characteristics,
the identity and system
for Année du Brésil en
France is able to show
the Brazilian festival by
rhythmic letterforms and
bold national colors.

The backside of printed
collateral is printed with
the simple three color
version of the identity.
The logo is recognizable
when broken into parts,
and energetic as a whole.
Typography is calm in con-
trast to the lively identity.

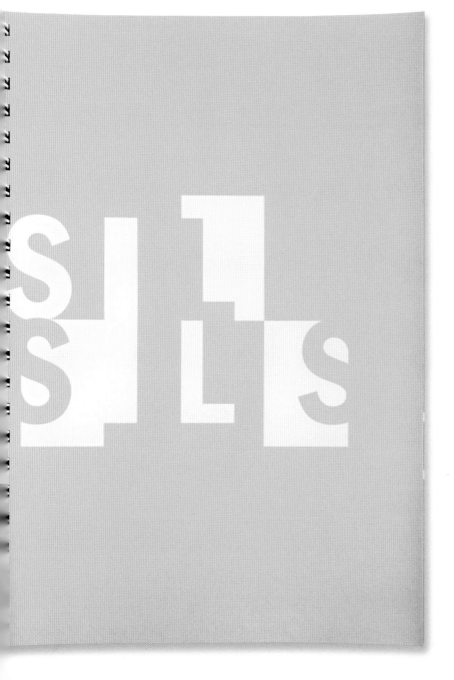

Advice for Identity Designers

1. Find a good concept to engage
the trust not only of the client, who
comes to a designer to solve its visual
communication problem, but also of
the huge mass of consumers. A logo
is a label of trust.

2. Simplify to reach the point where
the logo expresses the essential
without risking a poor design.

3. Create a memorable mark. A logo
is a sign of strength.

4. Achieve a logo that is easy to use,
especially on a small scale. Most
of the times a logo first appears are
in a small format: on business cards,
alongside a signature, or on a listing
of sponsors. In that context, a logo
must be easy to identify, to recognize.

5. Be flexible. A logo must be
flexible for its future uses, not too
strict, not too dry. It must be a point
of departure for future combinations
and brand extension. A logo must
be a timeless design. It must be
a robust construction, a crucial
economic force.

NUMBER SEVENTEEN

Emily Oberman and Bonnie Siegler
New York, New York, U.S.A.

Our First Logo
Ironically, the first logo we ever did was together. Right after we met, just out of college we took on a client together. We were not yet Number Seventeen; we were just Bonnie and Emily. Our client was a theater company called Stage Three. We did all their design for about a year, which included a logo. It was the word *stage* in Univers Condensed outline type with the word *three* in Futura Black in front of it. Unfortu-

HOMEMADE BABY ®

NATIONAL SEPTEMBER 11
MEMORIAL & MUSEUM
AT THE WORLD TRADE CENTER

SATURDAYNIGHTLIVE

WILLOUGHBY DESIGN GROUP

Ann Willoughby, Kansas City, Missouri, U.S.A.

Willoughby Design Group, Kansas City, Missouri, USA

At first glance, an identity designed by Ann Willoughby, founder of the Willoughby Design Group, appears simple, well crafted, and elegant. Upon closer inspection, however, it becomes clear that they are the cornerstones of a much larger structure. While some designers may focus on the form alone, and find pleasure in the crafting of a beautiful logo, Willoughby Design Group sees the bigger picture. The well-crafted logo is only one component of a larger branded experience.

OPPOSITE
Without ruining the playful original design, the new Wonder Bread design builds a clean distinct presentation of the identity that is again playfully applied to all sides of the packaging.

THIS PAGE
A bold new Asian inspired
boutique that sells branded goods and designer
collections required a look
as bold and memorable
to compete in the retail
world. Rather than
directly copying Asian
artifacts, the identity
and system incorporate
borrowed Asian influences
and contemporized art
with a Far East natural
color palette.

The retail space also has
a tea market that sells
loose teas and signatured
branded products. Without
overpowering the pack-
age design, the identity
maintains a memorable
system in the store and
when taken home.

Willoughby's first logo was used on a
"For Sale" sign for a local independent
realtor when she was fifteen years old.
From that noble beginning, she has built
one of the most internationally respected
design and branding firms. The Willoughby
Design Group's attitude toward identity
and brand is founded on Willoughby's
perspective that for any organization—
whether it's a nonprofit, a start-up, or a
well-established business—brand is about
reputation. "A logo and identity help
build brand equity, and if the enterprise is
successful over time, the brand (reputation)
becomes a more valuable asset," Willoughby
says. "A brand lives in the hearts and minds
of real people, through their experiences
and encounters with brands in daily life.
As these encounters become more targeted,
personal, and interactive, companies are
learning how to create more authentic,
meaningful experiences. Fortunately this
means opportunity for designers who can
design experiences that delight and engage."

The Bigger Picture
If logos amplify and clarify brands through
distinctive combinations of words, colors,
images, sounds, packaging, products,
service, and websites then the entire
response is designable. Willoughby believes
that a designer and a collaborative brand
team can shape the experience of a brand
and its content, meaning, products, and
services. As evidenced in Willoughby's
experience since 1978, current trends
indicate that people want more from brands;

sustainability, accountability, customization,
information, and convenience are some of
the many examples. While this process may
sound clinical, the end result is emotional.
"Our approach to identity helps people fall in
love with the brand through a kaleidoscope of
well-designed experiences," Willoughby says.

Willoughby's identity work is a combination
of simplicity, elegance, and wit. The simplicity
of the work exemplifies the idea that a logo
and visual identity program should express
a distinctive point of view and create a brand
strategy that resonates clearly in the context
of our visually cluttered world. The elegance
of the forms is, for Willoughby, a point of entry.
Beautifully crafted elements provide the
quality that is evidenced in all of the work
done by Willoughby Design Group. And finally,
the concept of wit is added to maintain a
degree of levity and to never let a logo sink
under the weight of its own importance.

But there is still a debate on the value
of symbols or icons over words. According
to Willoughby, symbols and color provide
a stronger connection to cognitive processes
than words. "Well-crafted pictorial symbols
are generally more memorable than abstract
symbols," she says. "If used, word marks
must contain distinctive pictorial elements
that aid memory."

SPIN!™

neapolitan pizza

SI GIRA, SI MANGIA, SI PIACE!

SPIN, EAT, ENJOY!

Umore Napoletano,

In the Neopolitan spirit; ➤We use our stone oven to roast every onion, mushroom, garlic clove, tomato, turkey breast, chicken sausage, artichoke and even croutons into the sweet and savory morsels that top your pizza ✎ We hand grate our cheeses ✎ We serve you only the quality of ingredients that we would serve our guests at home. **Buon appetito!**

Dine-in and Carryout	Catering Menu	Hours and Directions	email

Fountains Shopping Center | 6541 W. 119th Street | Overland Park, KS 66209 | 913-451-SPIN for Carryout

neapolitan pizza

THIS PAGE
The identity concept was taking the owner's two loves, Neapolitan Pizza and bicycling, and mixing them together as the basis for the logo and filter to what visuals would theme the open designed restaurant.

From the website to the dining room wall graphics, the system layered one color images to give a unique feel of motion, excitement and fun.

mary ✦ carol

ARTISAN PAINTS

MATTE FLAT

— INTERIOR LATEX —

scrubbable premium acrylic

heirloom tomato

1 US Gallon (3.785 Liters)

---

mary ✦ carol

ARTISAN PAINTS

MATTE FLAT

— INTERIOR LATEX —

scrubbable premium acrylic

molasses

1 US Gallon (3.785 Liters)

THIS SPREAD
The Mary Carol logo
has a "history" as opposed
to a clinical approach.
The packaging for Mary
Carol promote the
brand's message that
is warm and nurturing,
with a hometown feel,
while maintaining a
professional attitude.

Cross-Platform Thinking

Since forming Willoughby Design Group
almost thirty years ago, Willoughby has seen
a shift from mostly print-based work to more
screen-centric applications. Her work has
evolved to reflect the approach that logos
need to engage across multiple media. She
now approaches identity work as experience
design rather than traditional print graphic
design, and she has even let the change
in media inform her design process. Although
often not listed in an identity brief, Willoughby's
form-making process plans for animation
and includes working with an expanded
collaborative team of multimedia design
specialists. Media issues aside, however,
Willoughby maintains that the forms always
need to arise out of brand strategy and
meaning and deliver its desired emotional
triggers. Her process always starts with an
audit that unearths the character of the
company and its business and then moves
to identify all the places the logo might exist,
including the nuances of the specific media
and its audience. Once the parameters of
the identity are framed, Willoughby trusts
the design process to reveal the most beautiful
and delightful forms. These "aha" moments,
when the right idea emerges, tend to result
in marks that are strong, simple, and flexible.

Vision

But with the proliferation of new media as well
as the growth of branding experts, Willoughby
has also seen a down side. Logos and identity
design often becomes the misunderstood
stepchild of marketing and branding experts
without the benefit of the design process.
"We have all seen millions of dollars spent
on a beautiful logo and identity for a company
where there is a total disconnect between
the logo and the brand experience," Willoughby
says. "Trust and authenticity, essential to
successful brands, are qualities that often
have little to do with how much a logo costs.
In a perfect world, the logo and identity
are inspired by the founder's values, vision,
and entrepreneurial passion to build
something of lasting value."

Willoughby Design Group's work clearly
demonstrates a high caliber of expertise
across all media, and it has a timeless quality
regardless of the final application. But when
Willoughby discusses her favorite applications
for an identity project, she lights up. "We enjoy
retail environments where there is opportunity
to make a statement with the environment,
merchandising, products and packaging, and
signage," she says. To this end, Willoughby's
logos have also been applied to unexpected
places, such as a T-shirt promoting an eating
contest in Las Vegas. That's a long way from
corporate letterhead and high-end packaging.
"You just never know where your designs
might take you," Willoughby says.

TIVOL

TREASURED SINCE 1910℠

THIS SPREAD
A landmark Kansas City
luxury jewelry store known
for perfection in every
detail, the identity was
an extension of the
sophisticated shopping
experience they offered
to each customer. With
the identity as a solid
and simple voice, the
jewelry and timepieces
were able to stand out,
but still remain branded
in advertising, printed
collateral and packaging.

"A brand lives in the hearts and minds of real people, through their experiences and encounters with brands in daily life."

—Ann Willoughby, founder, Willoughby Design

THE
katalyst
CONSULTANCY

→ kevin carroll, katalyst
503.807.2401

pmb 341 • 9220 sw barbur blvd • #119
portland, oregon • 97219
kc@katalystconsultancy.com

What's *your* Red Rubber Ball ?!?

THIS SPREAD
Identities are not required to have the same expected elements. For Katalyst, the identity relies on like memories and human responses such as the feel of paper, texture of a rubber ball, or personal characteristics.

Business forms were printed on unrefined paper and labels for the address were hand placed on the letterhead to lend to the human experience.

Printed collateral, including special edition books, continued the identity system's tone and material. The *Rules of the Red Rubber Ball* book was the clients' signature story that "answered" the image choices of the other collateral.

Lucio LuZo Lazzara, Milan, Italy

Zetalab, Milan, Italy

Zetalab founder Lucio LuZo Lazzara is a global leader in the integration of logos, identity systems, and applications with multiple types of new media. Using the example of Steven Spielberg's *Minority Report*, he describes the contemporary environment: "I see new potential in entertainment, information design, and in the personalization of brands. The media are tending to integrate more and more with each other, and merge into a single instrument."

OPPOSITE
Design Pubblico identity is as multifaceted as the many programs it sponsors. Based on drawing templates, each event was given a signature icon as an extension of the main identity.

DESIGN PUBBLICO

THIS PAGE
The identity for Design Pubblico is black and white allowing the applications to utilize a vibrant color palette.

The system consists of a stencil typeface and specific colors for the types of events or venues. Red represents the Designers' House venue and green is used for the Pubblico site.

As our society consumes messages in Lazzara's words, "in a pan-medium," communication, advertising, and messaging become more challenging. The logo is the element that creates a unified message across these multiple mediums.

Identify and Define

The message vehicles used are becoming increasingly varied with the use of traditional media and nontraditional methods such as guerilla marketing and viral campaigns. For Lazzara, the logo must clearly and directly identify a company, a product, or an event. "This can be achieved in different ways," he says. "An identity can be narrative, it can be symbolic, it can be simply visually memorable, it can create a mood, or it can be minimal." The process to reach this solution begins with Zetalab identifying and understanding the real need of the client. This need often involves a logo and identity system, but when that is not the answer, Lazzara admits, "Sometimes we have even recommended to our clients that they not have a visual identity. It wasn't necessary."

The visual exploration includes a strong examination of the logo design in multiple settings, from an animation to a stencil on the street. "The future of the logo experience is, on one hand, an example like a tollbooth FastPass, which brings about the disappearance of the manual interface, as services will start to be automated," Lazzara explains. "On the other hand, entirely new media will be necessary with new functions and new requirements."

In the face of these forward-thinking concepts, Lazzara maintains that the core of logo design is still a problem-solving activity. The logo is the beginning of a communication. It is the signature of a wider system, a visual language. This system of different elements work together to solve the problem and communicate the message in any medium or setting.

Message, Medium, Marks

Following Lazzara's philosophy of multiple platform usage, and basic communication, he modifies the "Form follows function" maxim. "I believe that form follows function, and the 'form' issue by itself is not an issue at all," he says. His logos are varied in form and style, from simple to complex, from symbols to word marks. The solution is dictated by the message and the final medium. Similar in concept to Marshall McLuhan's phrase "the medium is the message," Lazzara's logos are designed with the belief that the application of the logo, the context of its environment, and the medium it uses are as important as the form of the logo itself.

"Failed identities reflect only the point of view of the designer," claims Lazzara. The logo and identity system must reflect the culture of the company, or they will not work. He also cites examples of failed logos that are too tight and limited. These are logos that are too static and are unable to animate or evolve in multiple media. Following the need for a varied use in an extremely complex and uncontrollable

THIS PAGE
Moleskine asked celebrated architects, artists, designers, illustrators and writers to fill their Moleskine notebooks with personal comments and ideas about the city they live in. The My Detour identity served as the focal point of the project and spread into a campaign in a range of mediums. Here, a promotional poster and detail above show the identity system including typeface usage, color and image style.

communication environment, Lazzara insists that logos that try to "tell everything" or solve a client's every communication problem will not succeed.

Pain and stress are typically part of a logo's release to outside creative partners, or an in-house department. Lazzara tries to keep the identity system under the control of Zetalab for as long as possible. He understands that someone else will eventually handle the logo. Each logo and identity system is designed to be flexible and consistent. In a multiplatform environment, this is the only possible solution to maintain a clear message. A singular, unchanging, inflexible identity may work in print, but it will fail in a broadcast setting. It may function on a fax form, but become banal and predictable on merchandise. Lazzara's elastic and fluid approach to logos produces successful and surprising applications in all media.

Holistic Values

The elements that are the backbone of Lazzara's identity system include a color palette, a relevant or custom designed typeface, image and illustration usage, and less traditional components. "To create a flexible and usable system, I also look at the rhythm created by voids and fills, textures, patterns, materials, and backgrounds," he says. Working with the logo, these elements create a singular message. The logo for the cultural association Esterni in Milan represents the meeting, the social interaction, the piazza, and Esterni's fundamental values. A flexible system of identifying marks was created to maintain consistent formal elements on many different applications. The system included color, typeface, and logo, but it also incorporated multiple identifying marks to create a constantly refreshed and vibrant attitude. Lazzara summarizes its success, and his core philosophy: "Don't think about a single logo. Think about a system."

THIS SPREAD
Identity graphic elements, limited colors and boxed typography are the key characteristics for the Milano Film Festival system. These choices enable the graphics to avoid any reproduction issues including low-end newsprint printing.

The graphic elements work as eye-catching, large-sized graphics, and can be scaled down to smaller sizes and with no problems of losing recognizable qualities.

The Critical Components of a Visual System
Logo
Color palette
Typeface palette
Texture palette
Pattern palette
Material palette
Background palette
Illustrations and photos usage

THIS SPREAD
The identity is consistent from year to year with only the simple change of numbers in the upper right circle. By doing so, the system graphics change each year, but the identity remains consistent.

The logo, strong illustrations, color palette, and typographic style create unity with multiple applications.

"An identity can be narrative, it can be symbolic, it can be simply visually memorable, it can create a mood, or it can be minimal."

—Lucio LuZo Lazzara, founder, Zetalab

STUDIODAVIDHILLMAN

David Hillman
London, United Kingdom

Advice for Successful Logo Design

To quote noted designer Bob Gill, "If you can't explain the idea over the phone, it's not worth doing."

OPPOSITE
Every Phaidon book is
published with the logo
on the lower corner of
the cover and consistently
placed on the spine.
These two characteristics
create a powerful
branding element that
is effortlessly memorable.

ABOVE
Using scale and dynamic
angles, the identity for
the Modernism exhibition
at the Victoria and Albert
Museum uses color, typog-
raphy, and form associated
with the Bauhaus.

"The element of magic
and creativity breathes
life into everything."

—David Hillman, founder, StudioDavidHillman

The **Guardian**

obongo

TOP
The Guardian's
bold, sans serif
identity immediately
conveys a sense of
urgency and strong,
confident reporting.

OPPOSITE
Editorial Intelligence,
www.editorialintelligence.
com, is a website that
sums up U.K. national
print publications each
day. It's an alarming

"Never give the client
what he expects."
—David Hillman

CONCRETE DESIGN COMMUNICATIONS

Diti Katona, Toronto, Ontario, Canada

Concrete Design Communications, Toronto, Ontario, Canada

Logo design requires a focused vision that uses large amounts of complex information and funnels that into a clear message. Concrete Design Communications partner Diti Katona has created a body of work that is connected with a philosophy that makes more with less. She designs a logo and identity project by distilling the message into a simple visual. "Generally, we think that successful logos should express as much as possible with the greatest economy of form," she explains.

OPPOSITE
Even cropped and as a background, the Masterfile identity is recognizable. Together with the photography it represents, both gain recognition and value.

Masterfile

this is our logo

Masterfile

This approach is made successful not by simply making a logo minimal. It is successful due to Katona's skill at slowly condensing a client's message, politics, business goals, and audience into a seemingly obvious solution. Understanding the client's culture and the audience's culture is at the core of every Concrete solution.

Form and Function

The goal of every logo and identity system is to create an outcome that makes a business successful. The aesthetics and form are critical, but they are secondary to the final business goals. It is easy to fall in love with a specific shape or color, and Katona is no different than any other designer in that respect. She has the ability, however, to set that aside, understand the larger issues, and modify the forms successfully to reach the desired business goals. "Designers have a tendency to try to make the logo say too much," Katona says. "You cannot communicate a company's product/service offering, vision, intended audience, and aspirations in a single graphic form, at least not explicitly. A successful logo needs to choose a singular message and express it clearly."

The logo must have a clear message, but this cannot happen without well-designed visual forms. Katona believes that most logos fail due to poor execution. She adamantly rejects the devaluation of skill. "In recent years, so much emphasis in design has been placed on 'concept,' that often the articulation of the logo, the artisanship, has been neglected,"

she explains. "Logos often have very simple ideas behind them. They need to because of the issues we've discussed. But what makes them work, what makes them come alive, is the way they are crafted. Often, the most successful logos are the ones that have a very simple idea, brilliantly executed." Katona uses the example of a project that involved collaboration with an advertising agency. The agency had developed the concept (the heavy lifting so to speak), but they needed help to give form to it. The implication given to Katona was that most of the hard work had been done and the only part remaining was to make the logo look pretty. However, the reality was that very little had been done. The concept had used very predictable symbolism. "While this may not have been the wrong symbol, it needed to be direct and easily understandable. Its predictability required a distinctive way of articulating the concept," Katona says. The crafting of a unique graphic form would distinguish this particular logo from the thousands of others that used similar themes. This logo succeeded in the end due to Katona's unique vision and insistence on perfection of form.

Signs and Symbols

For Katona, symbols can often have more power than a name because they use visual imagery rather than the alphabet. The symbol can be much more expressive. A picture of an apple, for instance, is instantly more recognizable than the word *apple*. "I still remember the time when my children were very young, well before they were able to read,

> ## "When designing a logo, distill, distill, distill, distill, and distill."
> —**Diti Katona, partner, Concrete Design Communications**

THIS SPREAD
At first, the identity for Masterfile looks as if it's just a standard typeface, but at a closer glance you realize that the letterforms are a unique typeface.

The identity system and execution of the promotional collateral are more free and open. Therefore, the quality of each piece is dependent on the designer.

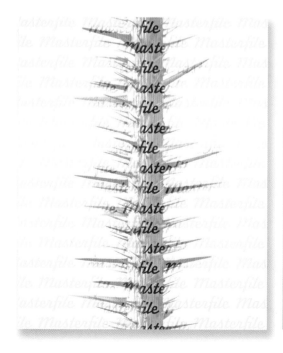

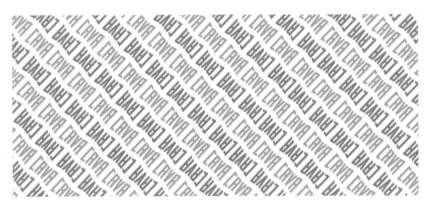

recognizing that McDonalds was a brand. The simplicity of the golden arches was all that was needed to communicate to them," Katona recalls.

Katona's philosophy on complexity and simplicity is pragmatic. For her, a logo should ultimately be whatever it needs to be to communicate effectively. The context and the communications criteria should dictate what form the logo should take. "Not the other way around," she clarifies. In the past, logos designed by Concrete were fairly simple in form. This was partly due to Katona's bias for simple and direct ways of communicating. In recent years, she has been exploring identities that are more complex and more reliant on color. Technological advances in reproduction influenced this. "Not very long ago, logos were designed for the lowest common denominator of reproduction processes," Katona says. "This, of course, meant the dreaded fax, along with other black and white applications. But with the pervasiveness of color reproduction, having it 'work in black and white' is no longer the prevailing mantra."

The shift in technologies, from a print-based solution to a multiplatform solution has affected Katona's approach to logo design. The result has been logos with more dimensionality and more reliance on color to tell the story. However, while keeping these influences in mind, Katona believes strongly that while important, these should never dictate the design. "Just because you can have a three-dimensional, spinning logo, doesn't mean you *should* have one," she jokes. Once the identity leaves Katona's hands, the unexpected will happen. Her strong standards for a color palette and typography will help the identity maintain a consistent look in multiple hands.

Formally, Katona's logos tell stories. The color conveys an idea. And, while often forgotten, or ignored, Katona always addresses the typographic system. For her, colors are relatively easy to specify, but typography is much more challenging. "Specifying font families isn't sufficient," she explains. "Type treatments, including hierarchy, relative sizes, and case, provide so many variables that very specific guidelines are critical for a consistent look."

OPPOSITE
Pulling from opposite sides like its rustic modernized European influenced food, Cava visually identifies itself with interpretations of 1930s dining graphics that are flat, but made contemporary by dimensional perspectives.

THIS PAGE
& NEXT SPREAD
An established Italian restaurant since 1963, the Pizza Nova identity is constructed with a primary word mark and a decorative script listing all the menu items in the restaurant. At a larger scale size, the script becomes a secondary graphic. From packaging, wrapping paper, website graphics, the Pizza Nova identity is exciting and tasty at a variety of sizes.

PIZZA NOVA®

1999 COLLECTION

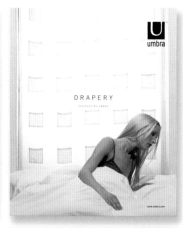

DRAPERY

THIS PAGE
Umbra is an
international leader
in casual, contemporary
designed products for
the home, the identity
reflects the design
approach with simple
and elegant shapes.
Somewhat neutral,
the identity is able
to present the
products without
being overpowering.

OH CHAIR

DESIGNED BY KARIM RASHID

www.umbra.com

KEILHAUER

Police Work

The elements of an identity designed by Katona are explained and described in a standards manual. "It helps if you can keep working with the client, and handle all of their communications," she advises. "Failing that, the success of any system depends on having a person within the organization champion the cause of adherence to identity guidelines. This person needs to be fairly senior with the authority to enforce the standards." This advice is not given to create restrictions on other users. When it comes to graphic communication, creative partners often resist rules and have a natural impulse to be "creative" with the brand. But it is vital that they understand that this impulse does not benefit the organization. "A consistent identity system may become boring to those who work with it every day, but is vital to portraying a strong image to the outside world," Katona says.

The consistent use of a logo and identity system, strategic goals, and business issues partnered with Concrete's thinking and visual skill create proprietary and successful brands. Katona, nevertheless, has a passion and humor that inform all of her work. In terms of logo and identity, this is expressed with her choice of a favorite application to design. "I love designing for vehicles," she says. "It's a great feeling to pass a logo you designed somewhere on the road." She adds that the strangest place a Concrete designed logo has appeared was on a homeless person. "Company logos printed on T-shirts invariably end up in the hands of a very unintended audience," she says.

THIS PAGE
Most creative work starts with a designer's first sketches. This Keilhauer identity celebrates the first sketch and relationship to the end final design. Several variations of the logo exist to work with different applications and varying sizes.

LOGO GALLERY

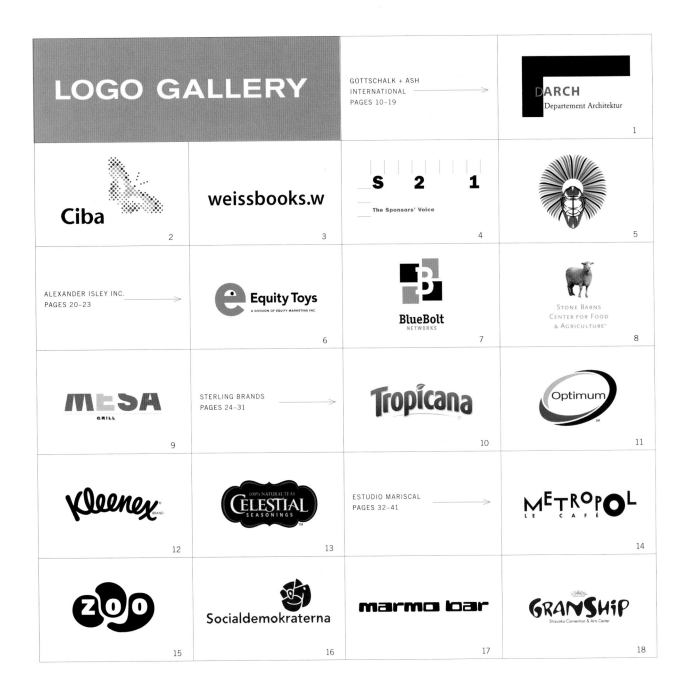

GOTTSCHALK + ASH INTERNATIONAL → PAGES 10–19

D ARCH
Departement Architektur

1

Ciba

2

weissbooks.w

3

S 2 1
The Sponsors' Voice

4

5

ALEXANDER ISLEY INC. → PAGES 20–23

e Equity Toys
A DIVISION OF EQUITY MARKETING INC.

6

B
BlueBolt
NETWORKS

7

STONE BARNS
CENTER FOR FOOD
& AGRICULTURE™

8

MESA
GRILL

9

STERLING BRANDS → PAGES 24–31

Tropicana

10

Optimum
SM

11

Kleenex
BRAND

12

100% NATURAL TEAS
CELESTIAL
SEASONINGS™

13

ESTUDIO MARISCAL → PAGES 32–41

METROPOL
LE CAFÉ

14

ZOO

15

Socialdemokraterna

16

marmo bar

17

GRANSHIP
Shizuoka Convention & Arts Center

18

Gottschalk + Ash International
1 Departement Architektur
2 ProLitteris
3 Implenia, Ice Hockey Palace
4 S21
5 IIHF 100

Alexander Isley Inc.
6 Equity Toys
7 BlueBolt Networks
8 Stone Barns Center for Food and Agriculture
9 Mesa Grill

Sterling Brands
10 Tropicana
11 Optimum
12 Kleenex
13 Celestial Seasonings

Estudio Mariscal
14 Metropol le Café
15 Zoo de Barcelona
16 Swedish Socialist Party
17 Marmo Bar
18 Granship

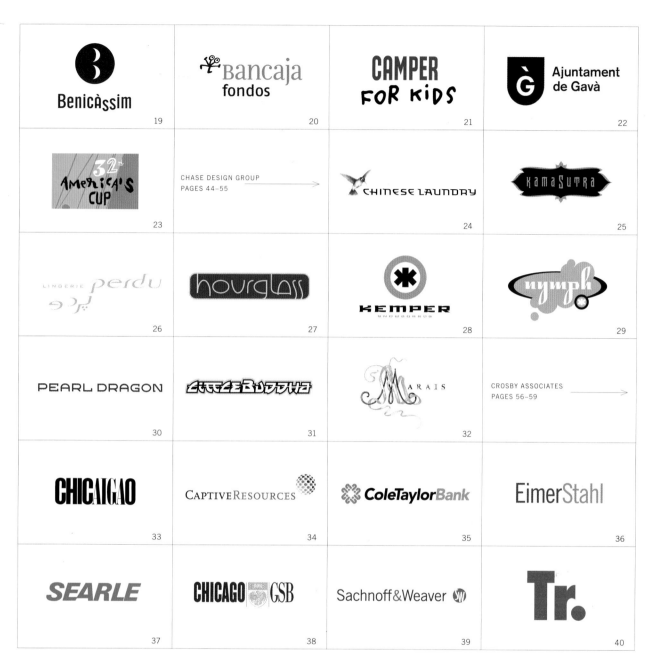

Benicàssim 19	**Bancaja** fondos 20	**CAMPER FOR KIDS** 21	**Ajuntament de Gavà** 22
AMERICA'S CUP 32 23	CHASE DESIGN GROUP PAGES 44–55	CHINESE LAUNDRY 24	KAMA SUTRA 25
LINGERIE perdu fee 26	hourglass 27	KEMPER SNOWBOARDS 28	nymph 29
PEARL DRAGON 30	LITTLE BUDDHA 31	MARAIS 32	CROSBY ASSOCIATES PAGES 56–59
CHICAIGAO 33	CAPTIVE RESOURCES 34	Cole Taylor Bank 35	EimerStahl 36
SEARLE 37	CHICAGO GSB 38	Sachnoff & Weaver 39	Tr. 40

Estudio Mariscal (cont.)
19 Benicàssim
20 Bancaja
21 Camper for Kids
22 Ajuntament de Gavà
23 32nd America's Cup

Chase Design Group
24 Chinese Laundry
25 Kamasutra
26 Perdu
27 Hourglass
28 Kemper Snowboards
29 Nymph
30 Pearl Dragon
31 Little Buddha
32 Marais

Crosby Associates
33 AIGA Chicago
34 Captive Resources
35 Cole Taylor Bank
36 Eimer Stahl
37 Searle
38 Chicago GSB
39 Sachnoff & Weaver
40 Tr.

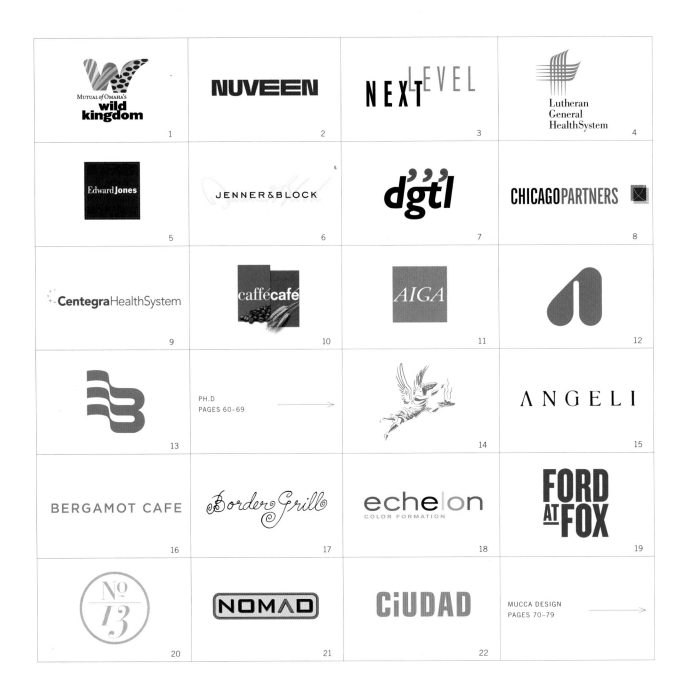

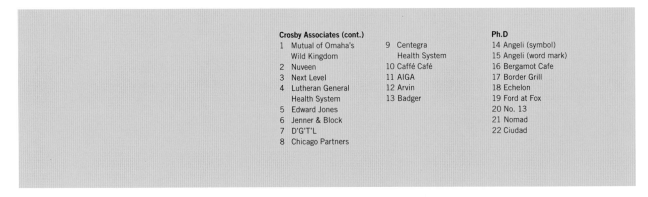

Crosby Associates (cont.)

1 Mutual of Omaha's
  Wild Kingdom
2 Nuveen
3 Next Level
4 Lutheran General
  Health System
5 Edward Jones
6 Jenner & Block
7 D'G'T'L
8 Chicago Partners

9 Centegra
  Health System
10 Caffé Café
11 AIGA
12 Arvin
13 Badger

Ph.D

14 Angeli (symbol)
15 Angeli (word mark)
16 Bergamot Cafe
17 Border Grill
18 Echelon
19 Ford at Fox
20 No. 13
21 Nomad
22 Ciudad

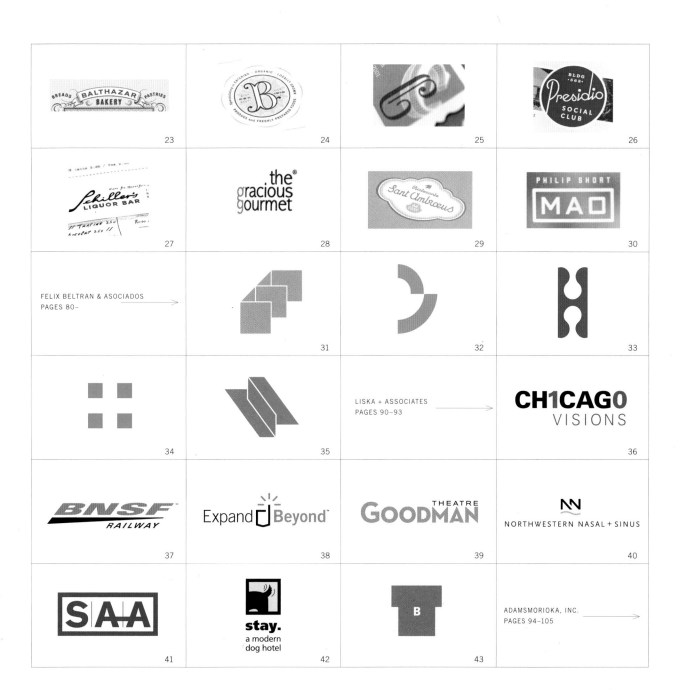

FELIX BELTRAN & ASOCIADOS
PAGES 80–

LISKA + ASSOCIATES
PAGES 90–93

ADAMSMORIOKA, INC.
PAGES 94–105

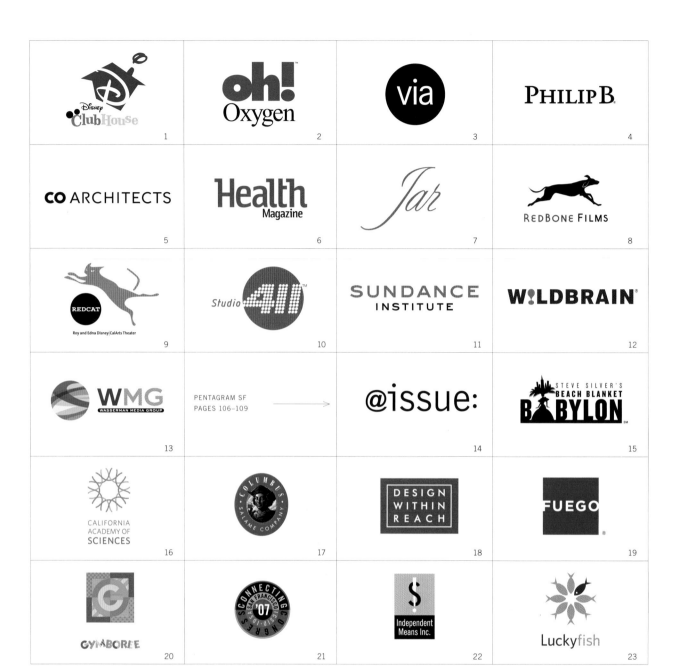

PENTAGRAM SF
PAGES 106–109 →

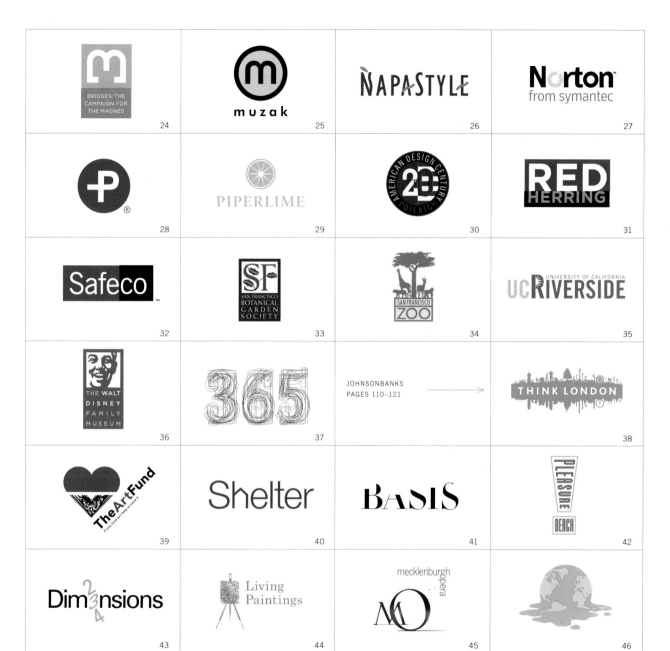

JOHNSONBANKS
PAGES 110–121 →

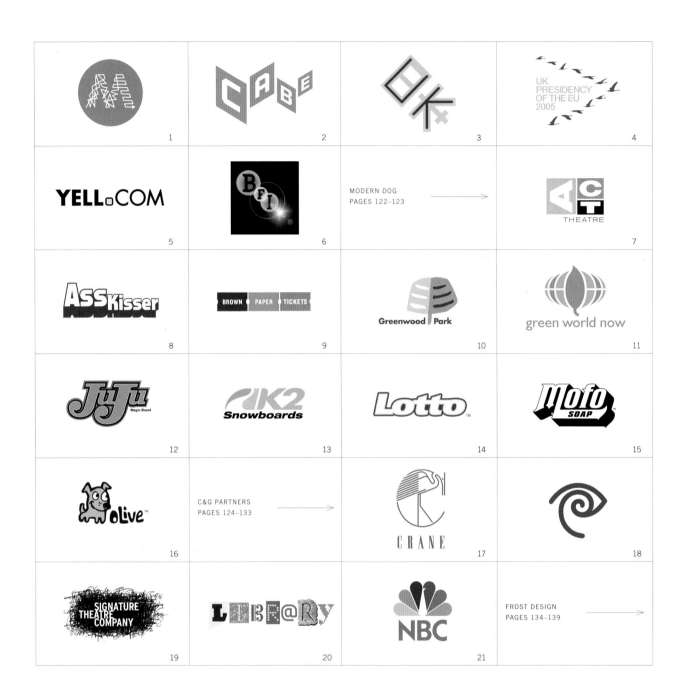

MODERN DOG
PAGES 122–123

C&G PARTNERS
PAGES 124–133

FROST DESIGN
PAGES 134–139

54
22

adq
23

Australian DESIGN AWARD
24

[V] CHANNEL ™
25

Boot
26

COAST
27

FRANCO&CO
28

freestyle
29

GLASS WORKS
30

IMAGE SOURCE
31

INTER NAT ER FASHION AL GROUP
32

SYD A N C E Y COMPANY
33

SYDNEY OPERA HOUSE
34

T R II O
35

tyo ™
36

CR EAT
37

KHAI LIEW
38

LAURENCE KING PUBLISHING LTD
39

THE LONDON DESIGN FESTIVAL 2003
40

MANTA
41

Swiss Re
Centre for Global Dialogue
42

IMADESIGN CORP.
PAGES 140–149
→

атлас люкс
43

CCB
44

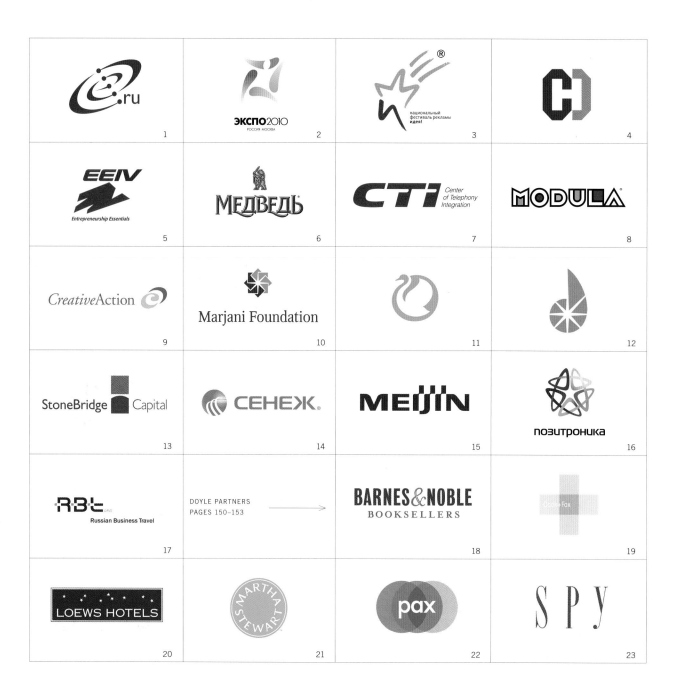

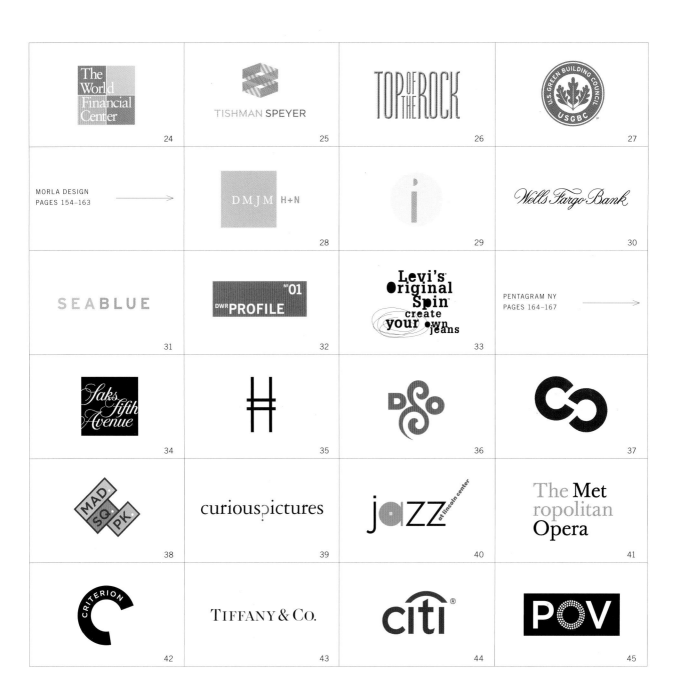

MORLA DESIGN
PAGES 154–163 →

PENTAGRAM NY
PAGES 164–167 →

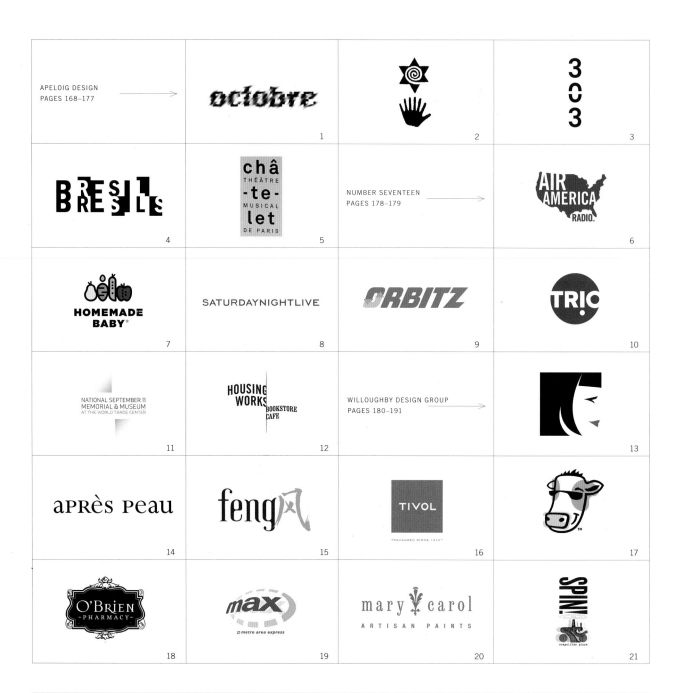

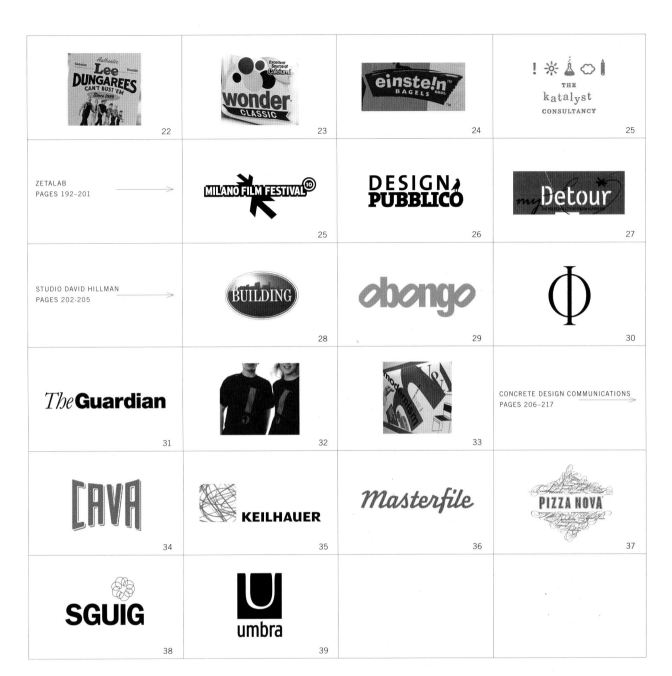

22	23	24	25
ZETALAB PAGES 192–201 →	25	26	27
STUDIO DAVID HILLMAN PAGES 202-205 →	28	29	30
31	32	33	CONCRETE DESIGN COMMUNICATIONS PAGES 206–217 →
34	35	36	37
38	39		

DIRECTORY OF CONTRIBUTORS

Sean Adams
AdamsMorioka
8484 Wilshire Boulevard, suite 600
Beverly Hills, CA 90211
U.S.A.
323.966.5990
www.adamsmorioka.com

Bart Crosby
Crosby Associates
203 North Wabash Avenue, suite 200
Chicago, IL 60601
U.S.A.
312.346.2900
www.crosbyassociates.com

Fritz Gottschalk
Gottschalk + Ash International
Böcklinstrasse 26, Postfach 1711
8032 Zürich
Switzerland
41 44 382 1850
www.gplusa.com

Felix Beltran
Felix Beltran & Asociados
Apartado Postal-M 10733
Mexico City 06000 DF
Mexico

Stephen Doyle
Doyle Partners
1123 Broadway, 6th floor
New York, NY 10010
U.S.A.
212.463.8787
www.doylepartners.com

David Hillman
Studio David Hillman Ltd
Unit 100, Pall Mall Deposit
124-128 Barlby Road
North Kensington,
London W10 6BL
United Kingdom
44.(0)20.8960.1717
www.studiodavidhillman.com

Michael Bierut
Pentagram Design
204 Fifth Avenue
New York, NY 10010
U.S.A.
212.683.7000
www.pentagram.com

Vince Frost
Frost Design
15 Foster Street, level 1
Surry Hills, New South Wales 2010
Australia
61.2.9280.4233
www.frostdesign.com.au

Kit Hinrichs
Pentagram
387 Tehama Street
San Francisco CA 94103
U.S.A.
415.896.0499
www.pentagram.com

Matteo Bologna
Mucca Design Corp.
568 Broadway, suite 504
New York, NY 10012
U.S.A.
212.965.9821
www.muccadesign.com

Steff Geissbuhler
C&G Partners
116 East 16 Street
New York, NY 10003-3034
U.S.A.
212.532.4460
www.cgpartnersllc.com

Michael Hodgson
Ph.D
1524A Cloverfield Boulevard
Santa Monica, CA 90404
U.S.A.
310.829.0900
www.phdla.com

Margo Chase
Margo Chase Design
2019 Riverside Dr.
Los Angeles, CA 90039
U.S.A.
323.668.1055
www.chasedesigngroup.com

Alexander Isley
Alexander Isley Inc.
9 Brookside Place
Redding, CT 06896
U.S.A.
203.544.9692
info@alexanderisley.com
www.alexanderisley.com

Michael Johnson
Johnson Banks Design
Crescent Lane
Clapham, London SW4 9RW
United Kingdom
44.020.7587.6400
www.johnsonbanks.co.uk

Javier Mariscal
Estudio Mariscal
Pellaires 30-38
08019 Barcelona
Spain
34.933.036.940
www.mariscal.com

Paula Scher
Pentagram Design
204 Fifth Avenue
New York, NY 10010
U.S.A.
212.683.7000
www.pentagram.com

Erken Kagarov
Imadesign
Russia
+7.495.775.4810
+7.495.729.5693
www.imadesign.ru

Debbie Millman
Sterling Brands
Empire State Building, 17th Floor
New York, NY 10118
U.S.A.
212.329.4600
www.sterlingbrands.com

Ann Willoughby
Willoughby Design Group
602 Westport Road
Kansas City, MO 64111
U.S.A.
816.561.4189
www.willoughbydesign.com

Diti Katona
Concrete Design Communication
2 Silver Avenue
Toronto, Ontario M6R 3A2
Canada
416.534.9960
www.concrete.ca

Jennifer Morla
Morla Design Inc
1008A Pennsylvania Avenue
San Francisco, CA 94107
U.S.A.
415.543.6548
www.morladesign.com

Lucio LuZo Lazzara
Zetalab
via Tadino 29/a
20124 Milano
Italy
39.02.29.533.992
www.zetalab.com

Emily Oberman & Bonnie Siegler
Number Seventeen
285 West Broadway, Room 650
New York, NY 10013
U.S.A.
212.966.9395
www.number17.com

Steve Liska
Liska + Associates Inc.
515 North State Street, 23rd Floor
Chicago, IL 60610-4322
U.S.A.
312.644.4400
www.liska.com

Robynne Raye & Michael Stassburger
Modern Dog Design Co.
7903 Greenwood Avenue North
Seattle, WA 98103
U.S.A.
206.789.7667
www.moderndog.com

BIBLIOGRAPHY

Adams, Sean, Noreen Morioka, and Terry Stone. *Logo Design Workbook.* Gloucester, MA: Rockport Publishers, 2004.

Chermayeff, Ivan, Tom Geismar, and Steff Geissbuhler. *TM: Trademarks Designed by Chermayeff & Geismar.* New York: Princeton Architectural Press, 2000.

Chermayeff, Ivan, Tom Geismar, and Steff Geissbuhler. *Designing.* New York: Graphis Press, 2003.

Dondis, Donis A. *A Primer of Visual Literacy.* Cambridge, MA: MIT Press, 1973.

Fella, Edward. *Letters on America.* New York: Princeton Architectural Press, 2000.

Friedman, Mildred, Editor. *Graphic Design in America: A Visual Language History.* New York: Abrams, 1989.

Gardner, Bill, and Cathy Fishel. *LogoLounge: 2,000 International Identities by Leading Designers.* Gloucester, MA: Rockport Publishers, 2003.

Halberstam, David. *The Fifties.* New York: Ballantine Books, 1994.

Hall, Peter, and Michael Bierut, Editors. *Tibor Kalman, Perverse Optimist.* New York: Princeton Architectural Press, 1998.

Heller, Steven. *Paul Rand.* London: Phaidon Press, 1999.

Hess, Dick, and Marion Muller. *Dorfsman & CBS.* New York: American Showcase, 1987.

Jacobson, Egbert, Editor. *Trademark Design.* Chicago: Paul Theobald, 1952.

Jaspert, W. Pincus, W. Turner Berry, and A. F. Johnson. *The Encyclopaedia of Type Faces.* London: Blandford Press, 1953.

Johnson, Michael. *Problem Solved: A Primer in Design and Communication.* London: Phaidon Press, 2002.

Kirkham, Pat. *Charles and Ray Eames: Designers of the Twentieth Century.* Cambridge, MA: MIT Press, 1995.

Meggs, Philip B. *A History of Graphic Design* (Third Edition). New York: Wiley, 1998.

Meggs, Philip B. *Type and Image: The Language of Graphic Design.* New York: Wiley, 1992.

Moss, Marie Y. ® *Hello Everything!: 25 Years of Fun.* New York: Abrams, 2001.

Müller-Brockmann, J. *The Graphic Artist and His Design Problems.* New York: Hastings House, 1961.

Neuhart, John, Marilyn Neuhart, and Ray Eames. *Eames Design: The Work of the Office of Charles and Ray Eames.* New York: Abrams, 1989.

Pentagram. *Pentagram* Book Five. New York: Monacelli Press, 1999.

Rosen, Ben. *The Corporate Search for Visual Identity.* New York: Van Nostrand Reinhold, 1970.

Tuckerman, Nancy, and Nancy Dunnan. *The Amy Vanderbilt Complete Book of Etiquette.* New York: Doubleday, 1995.

Wheeler, Alina. *Designing Brand Identity: A Complete Guide to Creating, Building, and Maintaining Strong Brands.* New York: Wiley, 2003.

Young, Doyald. *Logotypes & Letterforms: Handlettered Logotypes and Typographic Considerations.* New York: Design Press, 1993.

DEBBIE MILLMAN JE

BONNIE SIEGLER MICHAEL STRAS

WILLOUGHBY SEAN

CROSBY STEPHEN DOYLE VINCE F

ELOIG FELIX BELTRA

ALEXANDER ISLEY STEVE LISKA E

MARGO CHASE ST

ULA SCHER BONNIE SIEGLER MIC

RITZ GOTTSCHALK M

RUT BART CROSBY STEPHEN DO

CHAEL JOHNSON E

VID HILLMAN ALEXANDER ISLEY ST